Who's Sleeping with Your Husband?

A Woman's Guide to Rediscovery & Freedom

Dr. Jeri Godhigh

©2022 – Dr. Jeri Godhigh

Book editing and formatting by T&J Publishers
(www.TandJPublishers.com)

Cover Design and Chief Strategist
TVJ World, LLC
Franklin Lakes, NJ

ALL RIGHTS RESERVED
This book is protected under the copyright laws of the United States of America. This book may not be copied or reproduced or transmitted in any form or by any means, electronic or mechanical, including photocopying, recording, or by any information storge or retrieval system without the permission of the Publisher.

PUBLISHED BY

Josie's Girls Lead Company
3350 Riverwood Pkwy, Suite 1900, Atlanta, GA 30339
Phone: 888-413-7337 | Email: Info@jerigodhigh.com

Printed in the United States of America.
ISBN: 979-8-218-06684-0

www.Who'sSleepingWithYourHusband.com

I dedicate this book to my loving and fierce mother, the late Josephine Newman Thomas. Thank you mom for being courageous and tenacious enough to live your life out loud. You taught me how to fight and never give up! You also introduced me to the greatest gift, which is my Lord and Savior, Jesus the Christ. Mom, I will always love you!

"You are altogether beautiful, my darling; there is no flaw in you."

– Song of Songs 4:7

Table of Contents

Introduction: Who's That Woman In My Bed — 11

Chapter 1: Crushed But Not Broken — 17

Chapter 2: The Chains That Have You Bound — 29

Chapter 3: Your Place Of Refuge — 43

Chapter 4: Who Are You, Really? — 55

Chapter 5: Taking Care Of You — 67

Chapter 6: Sex In The City — 79

Chapter 7: Live Your Life — 91

Introduction
Who's That Woman In My Bed?

I CAN'T SAY WHAT TRIGGERED IT; ALL I KNOW IS I experienced a mental and emotional breakdown one day. Perhaps it was stress. I don't know. All I know is I was a wife; my life seemed to be going well. I had a nice car, a beautiful home, children, a wonderful husband, and many incredible blessings. So you would think that I would have been completely satisfied and content, especially when considering that I knew what it was like to be homeless and not have anywhere to call my own, to feel abandoned and alone. And yet, I was in crisis mode because I felt like I'd lost myself. I would later realize that maybe I never really knew myself. So, therefore, how could I lose what I never had?

I ended up staring into a mirror and wondering who

the woman was staring back at me. I needed to know who she was. I feared I would have lost everything I'd accumulated over the years if I didn't discover who she was. I would have lost my career, lost my family, and thrown away the life God blessed me with.

When you don't know who you are, you feel an emptiness that makes it difficult, if not impossible, to appreciate and enjoy where you are in life and what you have because material things were never designed to fill the void inside of you. For example, you might be married to the greatest man on the planet, but due to your lack of fulfillment you won't be able to accept his love fully. Why? It's because you don't love yourself. And how can you love yourself if you don't know yourself?

We often place unfair pressure on others to make us feel good about ourselves when it is our job as women to love and appreciate ourselves. A man can tell you a million times that you're beautiful, but if you don't know you're beautiful and believe you're ugly, his words will fall on deaf ears. You must know that you're beautiful because God made you that way. The job of building your self-esteem is yours, not another's. Once you give that job to someone else, you give that person complete power and control over you to shape you into what they want you to be. That is too much power to give anyone other than God.

I found myself in crisis mode, staring strangely at the woman staring back at me from the mirror because I'd never taken to time to share with you what I'm about to share with you in this book. I lived a life ruled by insecurity, fear, a negative self-image, misery and self-loathing. The result was that I made horrible choices, dated the wrong men, put up with

INTRODUCTION: WHO'S THAT WOMAN IN MY BED?

abuse, and ended up in places I never intended to go.

For years, I felt like an imposter, a fraud. I couldn't muster up the confidence I needed to face people and assert myself, the true person I was always meant to be. I wrestled with acknowledging my needs, let alone putting them ahead of other people's needs. I allowed myself to slip into the background until I became virtually invisible. And while doing so, I carried all of the gifts, talents, dreams, and passions, the potential and divine purpose God sent here with me. I hid from the world what God predestined for me to share with the world. And some people could see the gifts that lie inside. Some knew I had too much to offer than to sit back and be quiet, and they would encourage me to unleash my inner greatness, step out from the shadows of obscurity and give the world all I've got—don't die full; die empty! And I'd hear them and agree with them but wrestle with the thought of doing what they suggested. Before I could step out of my shell and make an impact on this world, I had to discover who I was first. Once I took the time to do that, I found my inner strength, I discovered the power I had, and no one had to push me to do what I needed to do because I'd recognized my greatness and began to push myself.

And now, I'm writing this book to let you know that the woman in the mirror is awesome; she's fierce; she's a lioness filled to the brim with great potential and untapped power. All you need to do is get to know her. Find out who she is. I'm here to help you do just that.

Now, this book isn't for the woman who is comfortable and content with where she is. It's not for the woman who isn't ready to take the inner journey of self-discovery so that she can unlock all that's within her. So, if you're that

WHO'S SLEEPING WITH YOUR HUSBAND?

woman who believes you've plateaued in life and there's nothing to add to you, nothing more to strive for, to accomplish, nothing more God has for you to do, and you are done, then I can't help you. But, I wouldn't ask you to waste your time either.

I'm here to appeal to the hungry woman, the curious woman, the one who feels like something is missing in her life despite what she possesses, and the one who knows she's yet to tap into her greatest potential and live her best life, and if you're that woman, hello. Welcome to the first day of your new life. I'm so delighted to meet you. And no, we don't have to be face to face. We don't even need to hear one another's voice over the telephone. I'm connecting with you through the pages of this book. I will share an abundance of life-changing revelations that will shift your mind and, ultimately, your life.

As I shared with you a moment ago, my life was on the wrong path. I was headed for a crisis of epic proportions. God intervened, thankfully, and now I'm here to be your intervention and wake-up call. Don't worry; I will walk with you the entire time we're together. Picture me holding your hand as we venture into an unknown land. Change is unknown. But it's also worth it. I'm going to challenge you to change the way you think, change the way you do things, change the people you associate with, change the words you say to yourself, and change the way you feel so that you can change your situation, circumstances and trajectory in life.

That is a good change. That is a needed change. It's time to change the woman you are so you can finally stop wondering about the woman sleeping in the bed next to your husband. And here's an interesting tip: The change in

INTRODUCTION: WHO'S THAT WOMAN IN MY BED?

you will set a chain reaction in your life and family. So get ready To Be Set Free!

One more thing: As you go through this book, I want to encourage you to take it slow. Don't be in a rush. Instead, go chapter by chapter and take the time to reflect on the current state of your life and digest the keys and revelations I will share with you. I would even encourage you to have handy a separate journal so you can write down your thoughts about the content you've just read. Trust me, that makes a huge difference and heightens the experience of going through this book.

Okay, that's enough talking. It's time to get moving. I sure hope you're ready to get started because I am. So come on, let's get going.

It is Time for You to REDISCOVER who you are and Truly Live Free to be You!

WHO'S SLEEPING WITH YOUR HUSBAND?

Chapter 1
Crushed But Not Broken

So you've been crushed; I know the feeling. I do. You've been burned, and now you hide your scars behind a fabricated smile. Perhaps you feel like life cheated you; it dealt you a bad hand. I understand. People told you as a little girl that you only get back what you dish out, so you dished out kindness, respect, love and acceptance only to get cruelty, disrespect, hatred and rejection in return. Now, you feel jaded, as if you were misled. Perhaps you now question whether or not there is any good in this world. I get it. I've been there.

Maybe someone robbed you of your innocence after raping or molesting you. Perhaps someone dragged your name through the mud and ruined your character in the eyes of others. Or maybe you lost everything you had; success, a thriving career, a wonderful home, a great relationship, money, all gone down the drain due to one bad decision or the actions of another. And now, you feel as if there is nothing worth living for and want to end it all; if that's you, we're speaking the same language. We both know what pain feels like. We both know what it feels like to be crushed.

To feel crushed is to feel devastated. Devastation leaves you heartbroken, lethargic, in a state of debilitating pain where it's hard to move at times, where it's difficult to get out of the bed and place one foot in front of the other. You feel depressed, even hopeless at times. And yet, you still get up somehow. You still slip on your clothes, wash and powder your face, fix your hair, throw on your heels and step out into the world, ready to take it on. You continue to look ahead to a brighter day, believing in love and the possibility of finding love. You haven't completely closed off your heart and shut down. You continue dreaming and imagine the opportunities that await you. It's easy to lie down and quit, but you didn't. You were crushed but not broken.

*

If there's one person that should be broken, it's me. I grew up in brokenness, and I was surrounded by it. I grew up with loss, experiencing the weight of emptiness in my soul. It started when I was around five years old when I lost my dad.

I grew up in the Washington, DC area, and in those times, everyone knew each other - our neighbors and sitting on the front porch was common. My parents worked hard to give me a good life. They did their best. They weren't married at the time of my birth, but they were preparing for mar-

CHAPTER 1: CRUSHED BUT NOT BROKEN

riage.

My dad owned a couple of liquor stores, and my mom worked for a telephone company. My dad made the mistake of getting in deep with the sharks: loan sharks. These were dangerous people. They would kill you if you failed to repay the money they loaned you. They would take out life insurance policies on their customers to ensure they got paid.

One day, my dad was checking out a property. He and my mom were preparing to get married. They were scoping out properties to settle down and start a life together. During this time, he was behind on his payments to the sharks.

While dad was driving to view a property, he had no idea he was being followed. While he was inside the property, the sharks followed him in. The authorities found my dad's body upstairs in the house, his corpse lying in a pool of blood. To this day, no one has been arrested for the crime we are aware of. The killers made it look like a simple break-in that went wrong.

After my dad's murder, my mom was devastated. And rightly so, as she was planning the wedding, which was to occur in a couple of weeks. The pain of loss and the pressure and stress of everyday life became too much for her. She had a hard time coping with everything that was happening. She felt it to be harder and harder to care for her little five-year-old girl. My aunt was a babysitter and watched children all the time. My aunt and uncle agreed to help my mother during this difficult time.

My mother had never been through anything like that before. She was crushed by the loss of the love of her life. And to lose him in such a devastating way made it worse.

WHO'S SLEEPING WITH YOUR HUSBAND?

She began to drink as a way to escape the pain. I thank God that my mother was a woman of God. She was trying to escape her pain, but God never left her alone. She even turned herself around and positively changed her life after the tragedy. While I stayed with my aunt and uncle, my mother took the opportunity to go back to school and further her career.

As a little girl witnessing my mother go through, I felt like my world was falling apart—and I hadn't even begun to live my life yet. I was still trying to wrap my head around the situation myself. One minute I talked to my dad, and the next, I was told he had just been murdered. I was now fatherless and motherless in a sense, trying to make sense of this chaotic world. I'd buried the pain of all of those losses in my heart. I worked on building a wall of callousness around my soul. Like many people who experience trauma, I did my best to block the reality of the pain I'd felt out of my mind. I didn't know how to process my pain, so I suppressed it. As I got older, I got good at suppressing things in my heart. But this can only work for so long. The things you try to suppress will eventually surface and cause you to become an emotional wreck.

*

As I mentioned earlier, I went to live with my aunt and uncle in Washington, DC. Every weekend, I would return home to spend time with my mom. I wanted to share with her how much I missed her, how desperately I wanted to stay with her and feel that close bond every daughter desires to have with her mom. It would take time and work to build on our relationship since so much had happened after my father's death. My mother was kind and giving; she would give me

CHAPTER 1: CRUSHED BUT NOT BROKEN

whatever she could to make me happy. But the one thing she had some difficulty in doing was being able to show love through being emotional and affectionate. My mother was the baby of 12 children. She wasn't given a lot of physical love when she was growing up, either. And you can imagine being the last of 12 children in the home, and your parents are worn out. Her mother was 45 years old when she was born, so she didn't get the type of attention she might have craved. So when it came to me, she had a hard time giving me something she had never received.

Because of my lack of receiving emotional love, and physical touch from my parents, I had a hard time showing love and affection towards others. At an early age, I retreated into a hardened shell and convinced myself that I didn't need love, and it was because of that attitude I often failed to share emotional love with my children. Perhaps I redefined love in those moments, accepting affection-less relationships as normal.

When I discovered the truth about love, I became determined to do things differently. Now, I didn't do everything correctly. I can't claim to have succeeded entirely in that area, but I made changes and took strides in the right direction. Furthermore, God has blessed me with another chance with my grandchildren. I am doing my best not to miss it this time around. And if you've struggled in this area, I pray you don't miss it either.

*

By the time I was a teenager, I was wild and out of control. I wasn't focusing academically, not like I should have been. A teenage girl with daddy-less issues, I was the perfect victim for boys looking to prey on insecure girls. I might as well have walked around with a giant "I" on my chest—the "I" is for "insecure". I had no idea who I was or wanted to be and had no direction in life. I was utterly lost. So, like so many girls who feel lost, I began chasing after the wrong things while seeking validation in my life. When a boy told me I was beautiful, then I felt beautiful. If a boy neglected or ignored me, I felt like I wasn't good enough. I longed for their attention.

My heart was desperate for love, although I'd told myself I didn't need it. But despite what I told myself, my tears kept falling during the midnight hours when no one else was around. I would soak my pillow with them. I would wonder why I was going through all of this. Why was my father murdered? Why did my mother go through so much? Furthermore, why couldn't I stop the bleeding in my heart and alleviate the pain and suffering I felt?

I'd gotten pregnant at the age of eighteen years old. Today, I can honestly say my daughter is a gift from God; she is one of the best things that ever happened to me. However, being out of control at the time, I didn't appreciate the gift of my daughter as I should have. I just wanted to live my life, to live for myself and continue to self-medicate with riotous living. I was dating all kinds of guys I shouldn't have, including drug dealers and men who did not mean me any good. After all, I had just graduated from high school.

Looking back, dating drug dealers was one of the dumbest things I could have done. When you think about it, it's no fun being with a guy who's paranoid all the time, looking over his shoulder for both the feds and those he's wronged who are looking for revenge. If you happen to be

CHAPTER 1: CRUSHED BUT NOT BROKEN

in the car with the dealer when his enemies exact revenge on him, you could get caught in the crossfire and lose your life. Or let's say your dealer boyfriend gets pulled over while having drugs on him; you may find yourself facing jail or prison. But I didn't care about those things at that time. I just enjoyed all of the things that came with that lifestyle. The money and the fast lifestyle can be addictive and blinding, but in the end, they always destroy your life and steal your soul.

GOD KNOWS

I should be dead; that's the truth. I put myself in too many dangerous situations all because I didn't deal with the issues of my heart. And how could I have? I didn't know anything about trauma, nor did those around me. The consensus in my home and community was: simply get over it whenever you hurt. People didn't talk about emotional healing; they didn't talk about mental health either. It was as if the topics of therapy and mental health were taboo. People simply ignored these things, drank, smoked, lived promiscuously and recklessly, and went on with their lives; that's like ignoring the check engine light on your car and continuing to drive it. Eventually, you'll find yourself on the side of the road, watching smoke billow into the air from the hood while asking yourself, "What happened?" You ignored the warning signs that something wasn't right and needed to be fixed; that's what happened.

God gives us warning signs. He'll cause the check engine light to flash in our lives. He'll even allow hardships and tragedies to strike us to get our attention and divert us from a greater danger. If we ignore these warning signs, we'll

WHO'S SLEEPING WITH YOUR HUSBAND?

inevitably experience brokenness up the road. It may take a wake-up call to get one's attention: a brush with death, an arrest, incarceration, the death of a close friend, the loss of a career or job, the threat of separation or divorce, and more. On a spiritual note, it might take a supernatural experience for some, such as a warning dream or vision, a spiritual visitation, or a prophetic warning from a man or woman of God.

God has different ways of getting our attention, and you will know it's just an attempt to get your attention when the very thing that crushed you didn't kill you. You're still here. You're still alive. You have the opportunity to get it right. You've been given a second chance.

God isn't trying to kill you; he's trying to heal you. Unfortunately, he can only get to some of us through pain and hardships. We won't even consider him when everything is going great in our lives. We don't pray until we're at our wit's end and facing a dire need. We keep trudging on without a care in the world, thinking our lives are set, believing we're in control, that is, until we find ourselves in situations we can't control, facing obstacles that are about to bury us. That's when we tend to think about God.

He has a plan for us. He knows what's up the road, what's waiting to devour us on the paths we're on. Unfortunately, we can't see these dangers; they're too far off for our eyes. Our intellects are too finite; our vision too shortsighted. You can't see that stray bullet that has your name on it. You can't see the car crash waiting for you up the street. You can't see the economic recession or depression that's around the corner. You think you have job security, but God sees that company folding two years from now and is trying to

CHAPTER 1: CRUSHED BUT NOT BROKEN

redirect your steps. You think you're safe, but God sees the dangers that await you and tries to divert you from them.

You have no idea what the devil has planned for you and your family, but God does, and he's trying to protect you from dangers you can't see.

Proverbs 21:2 declares, "A person may think their own ways are right, but the LORD weighs the heart" (NIV). Most of us tend to think we're smart enough and wise enough to cheat death and survive without God. We usually think we're right about everything; however, Solomon wrote, "The way of fools seems right to them, but the wise listen to advice" (Proverbs 12:15, NIV). In John 14:26, Jesus referred to the Holy Spirit, the third member of the Holy Trinity, as our "counselor." His job is to counsel and advise us, to steer us away from the traps the devil has set for us and guide us into the blessings God prepared for us. Unlike us, he has the foresight and insight to guide us effectively. But we have to be willing to seek him and follow his guidance.

When I think about the importance of following the Holy Spirit's guidance, I can't help but recall the events that occurred on September 11, 2001. We all remember the tragedy as terrorists highjacked planes and flew them into the World Trade Center towers and the Pentagon. Still, I remember the testimonies of people who said they were either warned by God in a dream or through a "word of knowledge" not to go to work that morning. Some people had that uneasy feeling in their spirits that warned them to stay home that day. One woman said the Lord spoke to her about her husband, who worked in one of the towers, and told her not to let him go to work that day. Looking for a way to prevent him from going to work that morning, she set his alarm

WHO'S SLEEPING WITH YOUR HUSBAND?

clock backwards several hours, causing him to get up late. By the time he'd awakened and realized what time it really was, the attacks were already underway. He watched in horror as the building he would have been in had he gone to work crumbled and collapsed, crushing and killing thousands of people. He would have been one of those victims had it not been for his wife heeding the guidance of the Holy Spirit.

On the road I was traveling, the devil had plenty of traps set for me. He wanted me to die in my sins while living promiscuously and running the streets with drug dealers chasing after money. It might have been a bullet for me or fatal disease. Who knows? God knew, and that's why he sounded the alarm to get my attention. He then pulled me off my path and placed my feet on a different one.

Despite the hardships that my mother had endured, she prayed for me; she introduced me to God, and for that, I am grateful. My mother loved the Lord. I could feel her prayers. She truly loved me, even though she didn't always show it physically. But the greatest act of love she could have shown towards me was to call my name out before God. She covered me in prayer. She cried out to God, asking him to protect her daughter. And He did just that. I will forever miss her and thank her for sacrificing her life for me.

Never stop praying for your family and loved ones. And while you're at it, never stop seeking God for yourself. As the Bible records,

> "The righteous cry out, and the LORD hears them; he delivers them from all their troubles. The LORD is close to the brokenhearted and saves those who are crushed in spirit." (Psalm34:17-18, NIV)

CHAPTER 1: CRUSHED BUT NOT BROKEN

That's the beautiful thing about the God I serve: he's alive and hears us. And not only that, but he answers those who call upon him. The way that he answers may vary, but he always responds. If your spirit has been crushed under the weight of life's many problems and burdens, God promises to fix it as only he can; that's his speciality. But you must call on him.

*

By the time I reached my early twenties, I'd say the Holy Spirit was reeling me in like a fish out of water. Finally, I was beginning to settle down and abandon the crazy lifestyle I'd gotten caught up in. Now, I was working and being a mother to my child. I didn't have time for much else nor tolerance for the drama and craziness I'd just come out of. God was growing me up. But I was still a mess.

By the age of twenty-five, I met my husband. I was still an emotional wreck, a traumatized young woman who didn't know how to love myself, let alone another. I still wrestled with insecurity as well as low self-esteem. I was beginning to know God, but I had a long way to go. I had baggage I didn't know how to dispose of or what to do with. I was like Erykah Badu's "Bag Lady," prone to run away from anyone who got too close to me because of the festering wounds in my soul I never got healed. But like I said before, I didn't know how to get healed.

It would take years for God to go through the stash of pent-up emotions and hidden hurts concealed in my heart, to wrestle the reigns of control over my life from my tight grip and bring me face to face with the issues I'd tried to deny for so many years. But, you see, God knew that my past trauma would be a roadblock preventing me from reaching my destiny in life, so He had to take me on a journey through the past to set me free. And it all started with breaking generational curses.

Chapter 2
The Chains That Have You Bound

"And you will know the truth, and the truth will set you free."—John 8:32, NLT

To move forward, sometimes, you have to go backwards. We try to move on with our lives as if everything is good after undergoing trauma, but this is a mistake. If you're not healed, that trauma will resurface at some point and derail any progress you've made. We hear about celebrities, movie stars, professional athletes, and the likes acting out in ways that place them in the headlines for all the wrong reasons—from suicide attempts to divorce to addictive behaviors. That is proof that trouble doesn't discriminate; it doesn't care about your socioeconomic status, where you live, what you drive, ethnicity, or gender. Many people are unhappy today because of the unresolved issues in their hearts.

Numerous online and in magazines have revealed that top models suffer from low self-esteem and body-shaming. While some girls look to these celebrities as the epitome of beauty, these celebrities are suffering in silence from complexes that make them believe they're ugly. They are dissatisfied with their bodies and hate how they look. In many cases, they develop eating disorders, have a hard time keeping food down due to bulimia, and crave outside validation. And sadly, no matter how much validation and praise they get from the outside world, it's never enough. They still feel empty and see themselves as not good enough, not attractive enough and not thin enough. I was seemingly unhappy with the way I looked. In my eyes, I was too big. All of my girlfriends were smaller than me. But if you look at my pictures from those days, you would quickly see that I wasn't big; Society claims that if you are thin, you are perfect. But it's all a façade.

That is the same problem that plagues the consummate business person who can't seem to earn enough money to satisfy and fill the emptiness in their heart. They also crave validation. Why? They need it. For many, money is a way to buy love, friendships, respect and acceptance. Without money, they feel unimportant. Many constantly wrestle with the thought of "I'm not enough" in their minds. Parents who were too hard on them may have made them feel this way. Some parents make their children believe they're only valuable and loved when they perform well and live up to their

CHAPTER 2: THE CHAINS THAT HAVE YOU BOUND

standards. We call these "conditions of worth." That, too, is traumatizing.

The point I'm driving home is that traumas lurk beneath the surface in most of our lives, leaving us feeling empty, lonely and desperate despite the stuff we acquire. We can't truly enjoy what we have when we don't know and love who we are. A new car, a big house, fancy clothes, a thriving business and a dream mate, won't make you feel better about yourself when trapped in the pain of the past. The burden of success could become a detriment. It isn't easy to heal while under the spotlight. Many people in this situation will attempt to appease fans and followers by pretending to have it all together, but this only places excessive pressure on them. Living in a fish bowl is a hard place to live. There is no place to hide! That is what happened to our family. We aren't famous or celebrities, but we were well-known within our communities and church. We were often looked at as the perfect family. It appeared that the Godhighs had it all and were the model family. Unfortunately, it is never all that appearances seem to be. We weren't perfect, our marriage was in trouble, and our kids struggled to keep up with "the appearance" and always be what others thought they were. Keeping a facade going will eventually wear you out. The Glass Fish Bowl will break if you aren't careful to do the work to keep up a good marriage, nurture your children and stay present in your lives at all times.

When your personal crises are made public, that exasperates the problem. Having your name flash across the headlines, having your pain trend on Twitter and social media, and having your troubles commented on by scores of people worldwide adds more trauma to the existing problem. It doesn't help when you're the butt of every joke when you look online and see people discussing your personal business, especially considering how cruel many people are. Reading the most hurtful and heartless comments about you online can be discouraging. Having the media blow up your personal life before the world and twist your words and deeds out of context to demonize you can leave you even more devastated than before; it adds an extra layer of embarrassment and shame. Unfortunately, many high-profile individuals would rather sacrifice their personal healing to save face and avoid that kind of humiliation. They fear losing people's respect, fans and supporters, and losing money, endorsements and television deals; this even happens to pastors, business leaders and professionals in the political and academic fields.

The spotlight is no place to air your dirty laundry and work on personal development; it isn't the proper place to grow up. It's easier to heal without the weight of so much pressure sitting on your shoulders; that way, you can focus only on yourself and not deal with so many distractions and outside forces.

*

I was in constant need of outside validation and couldn't understand why. I didn't know why it felt like a gaping hole in my heart was hemorrhaging blood, nor did I know what to do about it. I always felt empty inside, and like I mentioned before, that sense of emptiness drove me to make wrong decisions that landed me in places I didn't need to be and caused me to stumble into relationships I didn't need to be a part of.

CHAPTER 2: THE CHAINS THAT HAVE YOU BOUND

Your hurt and pain will subconsciously drive your life, influencing your choices, the people you connect with, and the outcomes or results you experience. Many of us question why we keep experiencing the same results in life, attracting the wrong kind of men, or why we continuously experience the same negative emotions. I'll tell you why: our pasts control our lives, and until we break free from the grip of the past, we'll never regain the power over our lives. But revisiting the past is something most of us choose not to do. We think we can skip forward and avoid resolving the things of yesterday as if they don't influence us, but that's now the case. If you're trapped in a pattern of doing the same things and getting the same undesirable results, realize that patterns don't just develop out of nowhere; they emerge at some point in our pasts and become habitual behaviors. These patterns have an origin, and finding their origin is the key to freedom.

THE ORIGINS

The answer to the questions, "Why am I the way that I am?" and "Why is my life the way it is?" was buried deep in my childhood upbringing. As mentioned in the previous chapter, I dealt with the trauma of a murdered father and many wrong choices and decisions. These things affected me more than I knew. They told me a story about myself. My father's murder created within me a sense of anxiety; I feared that anything I deemed special in my life could be taken away from me at any time. The fear of losing those who are most important to you can cause you to either cling to others too tightly or emotionally detach from others in an attempt to avoid feeling hurt by them. We avoid setting healthy boundaries in our lives for fear that these boundaries will drive certain people away; therefore, we allow people to walk all over us to keep them in our lives. That is one reason many women, including myself, remain in abusive relationships; we fear losing the men we love because we want to avoid the pain of loss and being alone.

It's typical for children to judge their worth by their parent's actions and responses. If a parent ignores their child, that child will grow up believing they are unworthy of attention, and that belief will cripple their ability to be assertive and destroy their self-worth. If a parent chooses a lover over their child, that child will believe they're not as important as other people, and as adults, they'll always place others' needs before their own and even disregard their needs as if theirs don't matter. Why do children formulate these ideas in response to their parents? It's because parents both mean the world to a child and represent the first authoritative voice in that child's life. That child looks to their parents for their identity. They need their parent's guidance. They also need to be affirmed by their parents—this lays the foundation for that child's self-perspective moving forward.

*

Are you in need of a hug? Do you feel something missing in your emotional world? You would be surprised at how true love and affection shown to you could change the way you act and react to things in your life.

We all long to receive affection from our parents, but this might be a far cry from what we may experience. And it's not necessarily our parents' fault because they simply live out what they've seen modeled before them growing up. What

CHAPTER 2: THE CHAINS THAT HAVE YOU BOUND

you may be looking at is a generational curse plaguing your family.

Let me stop and say for a second that the power of touch is extraordinary. Medical science has proven that touch releases endorphins and other healing chemicals in the body, which can lighten a person's mood, fight depression, and even increase physical and cognitive development in children, improving their mental and motor skills. Research has revealed that babies and children who tend not to experience the gentle and loving touch of a nurturer run the risk of stunted cognitive and physical growth; some have even died as a result. God designed touch for a reason. He even implored it repeatedly throughout the Bible, urging us to "touch and agree" whenever we were in need.

So as a child, I missed something I believed was crucial to my development, the touch. My mom held the same fear of loss that I did and sacrificed her well-being to keep me happy and close to her. However, since she'd never received affection, it was harder for her to give it to me.

As I studied my mother, I saw a pattern emerging. We operated with the same mentality, one that was passed down from generation to generation. Her mom may have been raised the same way; this is what we call in the Christian community a generational curse. Psychologists refer to it as a negative cycle of behavior.

Upon realizing this, I began to notice that I was doing the same things to my children that my mother did to me. I was depriving them of affection. I saw the same pattern happening to my children that happened to me. Finally, the lightbulb came on, and I realized I needed to change. Yes, I had to change! I needed to set a new precedent and example

35

and end this "curse".

I prefer to refer to this situation as a curse rather than a cycle for a reason. The concept of a curse carries a heavier implication and meaning; it entails a more spiritual, supernatural involvement in one's affairs. And I had to recognize that's what was happening with me. You see, there's a spiritual world all around us. The Bible tells us angels and demons surround us daily, and each of these entities has an assignment to our lives. God has assigned angels to us to lead and protect us, while Satan has assigned demons to us to keep us in chains of spiritual, psychological and even physical bondage. Have you ever wondered why families tend to repeat the same negative behaviors and experience the same negative results?

In one of the more famous cases, is it a coincidence that Bobby Christina died precisely as her mother, Whitney Houston? Is it a coincidence that Anna Nicole Smith died precisely like her idol, Marylin Monroe, while living in Marylin's old house? No! Some spirits have been assigned to families and individuals to cause them to repeat these mistakes.

DEALING WITH THE CURSE

Thankfully, we can break generational curses and change bad habits. You don't have to settle for something God didn't intend for you to have. But the key to breaking curses and negative habits is to recognize that you have them. You have to be honest with yourself and take a look in the mirror for once. Stop blaming others for where you are and examine your thoughts, actions, and beliefs—these are the things that placed you where you are in life, not others. You end up with

CHAPTER 2: THE CHAINS THAT HAVE YOU BOUND

that which you think you deserve. You only tolerate that which you believe you deserve. If you lack self-respect, you will tolerate disrespect. Suppose you lack boundaries and fail to train others on how they are to treat you. In that case, it's because you've convinced yourself that you need these people and that you can't live without them, or you've yet to overcome the trauma of abandonment that causes you to wallow in anxiety and the fear of loss. You fear being alone more than being mistreated, which is the problem. You think you are not good enough the way that you are and crave outside validation. You've been programmed with messages from the past that are designed to destroy your future. But all of this will change when you stop blaming others for your actions and outcomes and start focusing inward, looking at your negative habits and beliefs, and revisiting their origins.

The Holy Spirit is just the person to help you with this. He specializes in revealing to people the hidden things of the heart. Remember, the Bible says this regarding our hearts:

> "The human heart is the most deceitful of all things, and desperately wicked. Who really knows how bad it is?" (Jeremiah 17:9, NLT)

That means there are secrets hidden in your heart that you aren't even aware of. But nothing catches God by surprise. He sees everything, including the things you don't see inside you. And not only that, but He seeks to heal your heart; that entails being healed from trauma, psychological and emotional abuse, and even spiritual entanglements and demonic strongholds. Not only does God want to heal you, but He also wants you to "be whole," which means set free in every area of your life.

God desires to break your dependency on people, your people-pleasing addiction, your fear of rejection, your feelings of inadequacy and unworthiness, your obsession with others' opinions, and remove from you that sense of emptiness and loneliness and more. But you must first pray and ask the Holy Spirit to take an active role in your life and invite Him to heal your heart. Also, you have to be willing to face the truth about yourself. Believe me when I tell you that's one of the hardest things to do. Our pride often stands in the way. Pride will tell you that you don't have any areas of weakness in your life or trauma that need to be healed. It will lie to you and tell you that you don't have any shortcomings that need to be addressed. When you talk that way, you are implicitly stating you are perfect. If there's one truth that we can all agree on, it's that no one is perfect; all of us are sinners, groomed by iniquity and dysfunction; hence, all of us need correction and the Savior, Jesus Christ.

*

Discovering that you're under a curse is the first step. The next step is denouncing that curse. As the Bible states repeatedly, the power of life and death is in the tongue. Your words have power. Some of us have cursed ourselves with our tongues. For example, Proverbs 6:2 says, "You have been trapped by what you said, ensnared by the words of your mouth" (NIV). Don't agree with things that aren't a part of God's will for your life. Don't agree with the labels people place on you, especially those opposing that God calls you. Jesus said you must break agreement with these labels by

CHAPTER 2: THE CHAINS THAT HAVE YOU BOUND

declaring who and what God says you are. Joel 3:10 says, "Let the weak say, I am strong." It doesn't encourage us to agree with the labels: weakling, failure, incompetent, not good enough, unworthy, and inadequate. Call yourself that which God calls you. He professed that you are more than a conqueror, that you are the head and not the tail, above and not beneath, blessed and highly favored, wonderfully and fearfully made by Him, created by Him for every good work, and He said you could do all things through His power which He has called you to do. God called you an unstoppable force when you're connected to Him. Furthermore, Isaiah 53:5 says we were already healed of our sicknesses and diseases because of the stripes Jesus took upon His back and the blood that He shed on our behalves. You shouldn't claim sickness and defeat when you know that God has already healed you and has given you victory in every challenging situation you face.

Get up, tell Satan you will not die before your time, and stop agreeing with those demonic dreams, premonitions, and thoughts claiming you will die early. You must remind the devil that you are victorious and stop imagining yourself defeated. The only thing the devil can feed you are lies. He can't speak the truth. So resist any thought or idea in your head that suggests you are anything other than what God says you are. Change your words and come out of agreement with the enemy. Start agreeing with what God says about you.

For years, I agreed with the lies of Satan in my mind. I rehearsed those words in my head constantly. I called myself everything except what God called me, and as a result, I operated under an identity that wasn't mine and a curse

WHO'S SLEEPING WITH YOUR HUSBAND?

God never intended for me to have. And it wasn't until I got older that I discovered what was going on in my life and denounced that curse.

I want to invite you to experience the same power and freedom I experienced and break generational curses as I had. I want to bring you to that place through prayer. So let me pray for you now:

> Dear Heavenly Father, I thank you for sending your Son, Jesus the Christ, down here to earth to break every curse off of my life and heal my heart from every trauma and pain while setting me free from every form of bondage. As the Bible declares, whom the Son sets free, they are free indeed. You said we shall know the truth, and the truth shall make us free. Holy Spirit, the Bible calls you the Spirit of Truth. You are the one who guides all men into the truth, exposing the secrets of our hearts and the hidden works of the enemy. Holy Spirit, search out my heart and reveal every trauma and hindrance in my life. I surrender my heart to you. Also, reveal to me every agreement I've made with the enemy so I may denounce it. For I denounce and come out of agreement with everything the enemy has said about me. I break every covenant with the enemy I have established through ignorance or a deliberate act of mine. I surrender my life to you and ask you to seize complete control of my body, mind, soul and spirit. Reveal to me my true identity—my identity in Christ. Thank you for healing my heart, delivering me from the past and every

CHAPTER 2: THE CHAINS THAT HAVE YOU BOUND

trauma, and filling me with your love, peace, joy, power, self-control, patience, wisdom, and the assurance of my bright future. I forgive those who hurt me and release them into your hands. I pray this in Jesus' name, amen.

WHO'S SLEEPING WITH YOUR HUSBAND?

Chapter 3
Your Place Of Refuge

EVERY WOMAN WANTS TO FEEL SAFE IN A LOVER'S ARMS. We want the security of knowing our hearts are in good hands. When there's a strong sense of security, there is also a strong sense of trust. However, when we feel unsecured by our partners, we lack trust in them.

Many of us were taught that we are automatically supposed to trust everyone, but that's not true. We're supposed to love everyone, but that doesn't mean we are supposed to trust everyone. Trust is a valuable thing, something to be earned, not freely given. When you trust someone, you're opening your heart to them and giving them a place at the table. That should only be a privilege earned by those who've proven themselves worthy of that level of intimacy.

Even when it comes to God, we must earn intimacy with Him. God loves us all but doesn't trust everyone with

His blessings. We may ask for things, but only God knows if we possess the maturity to handle what we're asking for. A parent wouldn't trust their five-year-old son with a car; therefore, why would God trust an immature person with a big responsibility? He wouldn't! That is why Paul wrote in 1 Timothy 3:6 that those seeking leadership positions and elevation must not "[be a] novice, lest being lifted up with pride he fall into the condemnation of the devil." In other words, he said that a new convert to the faith doesn't possess the experience and the maturity to lead. The second they encounter a situation they're unprepared for, they will crumble or fold. And what is even worse is, the second they gain a great victory, they will allow that victory to go to their head and allow pride to destroy them from within.

Jesus said in John 15:15, "I no longer call you slaves, because a master doesn't confide in his slaves. Now you are my friends, since I have told you everything the Father told me" (NLT). He said intimacy with God is progressive: you graduate from the servant stage to the friend stage. It's in the friend stage that God shares with us secrets He won't share with others. But what allows us to reach this level of intimacy with God? He revealed it a few verses earlier when He said, "But if you remain in me and my words remain in you, you may ask for anything you want, and it will be granted" (John 15:7, NLT). Obedience to Christ's commandments and faithfulness to Him grants us greater levels of access to His presence. God will often test us to see if our hearts are truly in Him or if we're simply interested in what He can give us.

Like God, we shouldn't be so quick to give away our trust and open the doors of our hearts to just anyone. But

CHAPTER 3: YOUR PLACE OF REFUGE

whenever a woman is insecure, she will let her guard down and open the gates of her heart to the first guy that tells her she's pretty. She'll even use intimacy to win over a guy she knows means her no good. Her standards are too low; no guy feels like she's a catch; they walk all over her and use her. And sadly, once they're done using her, they discard her as if she's nothing. You are worthy, beautiful, and the catch that deserves to be loved in a special way. Never settle! You are too precious for that. I learned my lesson the hard way and will never make that mistake again. Get to know who you are and whose you are!

Make yourself a catch; make a man earn intimacy. Make him work for it. Don't just give it away like you are handing out candy. Instead, make it so that trust is too costly to throw away. Then, if that man knows trust is fragile and highly expensive, he'll think twice about tossing it away. Instead, he'll think about how hard he had to work to gain it. As Jesus explained in Luke 7:47, whenever a person places a greater level of investment into something, they'll value it more; they'll be more appreciative of what they've been given because they sacrificed more to receive it.

BROKEN COVENANTS

Now, let's talk about what happens when trust is broken. Because trust is so costly, it is devastating when violated. We must break through barriers of fear and anxiety, overcome hurdles of "what if?" and cross rivers of pain to put our hearts in the position to be vulnerable. That is especially true for those who've been burned and wounded before. Some of us are so guarded out of fear of being hurt again that it will take a miracle for us to let our guards down with someone. And after all of that sacrifice, after we've unbolted the doors, lifted the iron gates and lowered the drawbridge, and allowed that person to enter our hearts, they end up hurting us. They may cheat on us either physically or emotionally. For example, they might betray your trust by stealing from you and then taking off. Or they might betray your trust in other ways, like sharing your secrets with others, including their friends and family members. Such a betrayal can leave you feeling shattered. And yes, it can make you close the gates of your heart and vow never to open them again.

Broken trust tampers with your self-esteem; it causes us to question whether or not we were good enough for our partners. If your man cheats on you, these questions tend to lurk somewhere in the crevices of your mind: *What does that other woman have that I don't have? Why did he choose her? Was I not enough for him? Did I not fulfill his wishes and desires?* And worse is the constant pondering over the details of the affair: what was said, what was done, how the sex went, did he do things with the other woman that he wouldn't do with you, etc.?

Suppose your partner shares your secrets with others. In that case, this will leave you feeling paranoid, wondering what others think about you; it can make you uncomfortable around others and feel like you're constantly being judged. Judgements and criticism are soul-destroyers; they're designed to do one thing: make a person feel inadequate. We should all have a sense of pride and privacy, but we're left feeling humiliated when these things are taken away.

The worst part of this is the feeling of bitterness that usually follows broken trust. Bitterness becomes our wall of defense, our way of protecting ourselves from repeat offenses

CHAPTER 3: YOUR PLACE OF REFUGE

and attacks. So many of us have built walls around our hearts to keep marauders out, but those walls also operate as a prison that keeps us isolated, lonely and alone. Isolation is just as bad as a betrayal; it eats away at the mind like cancer, causing depression.

Yes, it's possible and doable to be happy while single, but not while isolated and alone. Even if you don't have a sexual partner in your life, you still need intimate relationships with others: friends and family members. You still need to form strong bonds with other people in other capacities. In the normal course of a day, you must trust someone. Think about it:

- You must trust the person cooking your food at the restaurant.
- You have to trust the doctor who's examining your body.
- You even have to trust the public officials asking for your social security number and the cashiers to whom you are handing your credit and debit cards.

You know the risks: a cashier could jot down your card number and then use it. An official could use your social security number and steal your identity. A cook or chef could do something terrible to your food. A doctor could take advantage of you while you are under anesthesia. And yet, you trust each of these persons. After all, you realize you need them to survive. Therefore, relationships are the currency of life. You need them. You can't survive while isolated.

However, bitterness leaves you isolated; it erodes your core and causes a stench of negativity to emanate from your pores. When you're bitter, you see everything through a negative lens, which then drives people away from you. That has the effect of causing more isolation in your life. And if you're not careful, you'll simply claim people are leaving your life because they're "haters" or because God is removing them from your life, when in reality, they're leaving because they can't stand to be in a fog of negativity all the time. Your attitude is that fog, and it can be suffocating to other people. Many of these people love you, but they can't stay around you while you're in your current state of mind.

Bitterness not only ruins your relationships and prevents you from experiencing love again but also blocks you from receiving God's blessings. Hebrews 12:14-15 says, "Work at living in peace with everyone, and work at living a holy life, for those who are not holy will not see the Lord. Look after each other so that none of you fails to receive the grace of God. Watch out that no poisonous root of bitterness grows up to trouble you, corrupting many" (NLT). Living at peace with others doesn't mean you support everything they do; it means you show the love of God to everyone. That doesn't mean you erase boundaries; it simply means you forgive and show mercy to people, and you seek to heal and deliver them from whatever bondage they're caught up in.
In some cases, this may mean praying for a person at a distance. You're still praying for them and believing for their best, healing, and salvation, although you've put distance between the two of you. God doesn't want you to stay in a situation where you're being abused. So you can still love someone from a distance.

Don't let bitterness settle in your heart and rob you of a future. Bitterness will whisper in your ear words like these: "You'll never find love again. No one is trustworthy." Its goal

CHAPTER 3: YOUR PLACE OF REFUGE

is to make you abandon all hope of experiencing a loving relationship. The truth is God has someone in store for you, but if you isolate yourself and harden your heart, you will miss God's blessing. You have to tell yourself God has the best for you. He does! He wants to guide you into greater and better things, but you have to be open to His guidance and don't sabotage yourself with inner vows such as these: "I will never love again. I'm going to remain single for the rest of my life. I cannot trust anyone." And be careful about making this inner vow: "I'm never going to let anyone hurt me again." I'll tell you why that declaration is so dangerous.

UNREALISTIC EXPECTATIONS

Choosing to remain isolated so you'll never be disappointed again is detrimental to your health, but what's even more damaging is holding unrealistic expectations of others and yourself. It doesn't matter how much you love someone; you will disappoint them at some point. Likewise, despite how much someone may love you, they will disappoint you. Why? Because people are only people. Every human is flawed. No one can be everything you need. No one can live a mistake-free life. People will sometimes say the wrong things despite their best wishes, fail to meet your expectations, forget to do the things you ask of them, and more. The people you hold to high expectations have the same flaws and shortcomings as you. And not only that, but they also have their own lives. They have other obligations to meet, stresses and cares of their own to deal with, internal issues they have to contend with behind closed doors, and more. Therefore, expecting perfection from a flawed individual is absurd. That is why God expects us to forgive others. He urges us to do this because we need that same forgiveness for our sins.

Forgiveness means you've chosen to forgive someone for a debt they owed you. God forgave us for the debt we owed Him and therefore expects us to extend that same grace to others. To do this, we must remember we're no better than those who hurt us. So think about the people you hurt. That proves that all of us need grace and mercy.

It is noteworthy to mention that just because you forgive someone doesn't mean the sting of their betrayal magically goes away. On the contrary, you will still feel the pain of that hurt. You may even continue to question yourself, wondering why your partner betrayed you. But this is what you must do to deal with the pain you feel:

STEPS TO HEALING

First, you need to acknowledge your pain. Don't invalidate how you feel. Realize that your emotions are important, worthy of recognition, and valid. Even if your emotions are wrong, they're still yours. Embrace them. Embrace your pain.

The biggest mistake many people make during this process is they try to erase how they feel. The problem with this is when you try to suppress your pain, it will eventually resurface elsewhere; it doesn't simply disappear. But when you acknowledge your pain and articulate how you feel, you will allow your heart to process that pain, decreasing its intensity.

Secondly, you must stop beating yourself up for someone else's actions and get the proper perspective of the situation. Realize that you are not responsible for anyone's

CHAPTER 3: YOUR PLACE OF REFUGE

actions but your own. In other words, you're not to blame for someone else's decisions. For example, if your relationship is on shaky ground and your partner cheats on you, that was a personal decision of theirs. Rather than try to repair the relationship, they decided to fall for the greener-grass syndrome.

Speaking of the greener-grass syndrome, everyone has flaws, so believing that things would be so much better with someone else is a delusion we believe. Oh! You remember the 80/20 rule? You will only find yourself leaving one problem for another. You're not going to find the perfect person. Sometimes, what you have is much better than what you're looking at, but you don't realize it. If you clean up what you have and invest in it, you might be surprised at what you have. But you have to understand that relationships take work; they're not going to maintain themselves any more than a car will change its own oil and filter. I once heard Evangelist Joyce Meyers say, "Don't be fooled by the notion that the grass is greener on the other side. You'll have to mow that lawn too." Take the time to focus on Yourself! You are more important than the problem!

Again, regarding getting the right perspective, realize that someone else's actions are not a reflection on you; they are a reflection on them. The child in you wants to ask, "What did I do to deserve this?" But your rational, mature adult brain intuitively responds to the situation by saying, "You are not responsible for other people's bad behavior. Everyman is responsible for their own actions." It's up to you which part of *you* you will listen to and believe.

Thirdly, realize that you can only make yourself get better. Your healing is your responsibility and not someone else's. If you give someone else the role of savior in your life, they'll control your life. The only one who deserves that role in your life is Jesus the Christ. You have to pursue your healing actively; you can't be apathetic. Attend counseling and group therapy sessions, read books on emotional healing and personal development, and most of all, attend church, prayer meetings, Bible studies, and more to connect with others that can help usher you into your healing. Yes, God does use people. Stop isolating yourself and focus on bettering yourself. You don't have to let disappointment or pain define you; you can allow it to become a teaching tool and a stepping stone. As the old saying goes: "Whatever doesn't kill you only makes you stronger." So grow stronger from this.

The fourth step is to take action towards rebuilding yourself and your relationship, should you choose to preserve it. The best way to rebuild a relationship ravished by infidelity is to attend couples counseling. It will take time because you must regain your trust in your partner, but it's worth it if the relationship is salvageable and valuable to you. Some couples grow stronger after experiencing infidelity and then recovering. So be prayerful and follow the Holy Spirit's guidance here. And even if the relationship doesn't survive, know that friendship is still possible, and it may be needed for the sake of your children if you have them.

Lastly, the thing that brings healing into your life is seeking to understand the other person. Understanding the cause behind a person's actions takes the sting out of their betrayal of trust. For example, if you discover that your partner has trust issues or a fear of commitment based on the fear of loss, you'll feel less guilty for their actions and realize it's they who have the problem. But not only that, but you'll also

CHAPTER 3: YOUR PLACE OF REFUGE

see them in a new light: rather than seeing them as a monster who came to steal your life and devour your soul, you'll perceive them as a fellow human being in desperate need of help. When you understand the person, you gain greater sympathy for them and learn how best to help them. Furthermore, you'll realize that it's not them who's hurting you; they're only doing what they know to do; they're only operating out of ignorance and being misled and wrongly influenced. Like the Bible says, "For we are not fighting against flesh-and-blood enemies, but against evil rulers and authorities of the unseen world, against mighty powers in this dark world, and against evil spirits in the heavenly places" (Ephesians 6:12, NLT). There's always a cause behind one's actions; according to the Scriptures, the source behind one's actions is spiritual. Knowing this, you're in a better position to deal with the situation, knowing that you're not the blame and the root cause is something far bigger than yourself. You'll realize there is a spiritual battle taking place.

Now, realize I'm not telling you to remain in an abusive relationship, especially to save face. Get out of that environment and get help right away! You can still pray for someone from a distance. You are more important than anything!

WHO'S SLEEPING WITH YOUR HUSBAND?

Chapter 4
Who Are You, Really?

MOST OF US HAVEN'T TAKEN THE TIME TO GET TO know ourselves. Instead, we spend every moment focusing on everyone but us. We focus on what other people think about us, their opinions of us, what they have to say about us, and how they feel about us, but sadly, we place little to no value on what we think and feel about ourselves. We're consumed with the thought of other people's wants and needs while ignoring our own. That is a problem.

Women who don't understand who they are and their value and worth tend to get lost in their relationships. What I mean by that is they allow themselves to be defined by their partners and society. Their boyfriends and husbands tell them who they are. For some women, their kids define who they are. They find themselves becoming everything for everyone, seeking to please everyone but themselves. They exist only to meet their partner's needs, and they allow their needs to go unmet. They lack standards and boundaries because they don't value themselves. Ask me how I know—I know because that was me!

Of course, they don't value themselves! How can you value yourself if you don't know who you are? So, in this chapter, I want to take you on a quest of self-discovery and get you to ask questions you probably never asked yourself, such as: *What is my purpose in life? What things about myself do I like? What are my strengths, talents, passions and goals in life? What makes me unique? What do I like in the bedroom? What do I want out of a relationship? What are my needs, and how can a partner best serve me? What's my love language? What do I enjoy doing when alone? What are my favorite activities, the things that bring me the most pleasure and fun? What are my deal-breakers in a relationship? What irks me, and what turns me on? How do I want to be treated and talked to?*

I want you to begin thinking about all of those questions and then take the time to examine yourself. If you've never asked yourself any of those questions before, it might be a challenge to you to answer them. Those questions will spark a world of internal dialogue, but that is what you want.

WHO YOU ARE NOT?

Before I go any further, I want to take a moment and clarify one thing: I want to remind you of who and what you're not. First of all, you are not your job! Whenever we meet someone new, we'll lead with this question: "What do you do?" Whenever people meet us for the first time, that is the question they usually ask us; this emphasizes our jobs and careers as that which define us. Those of us who've been led

CHAPTER 4: WHO ARE YOU, REALLY?

by society to believe our worth is wrapped up in what we do, where we live, what we drive, how much money we make, and what letters rest in front of or behind our names, we'll allow this question to cause us either great shame or let it inflate our egos and cause us great pride. If you don't have a great job and make a lot of money, you'll feel ashamed and attempt to divert the attention away from yourself. On the other hand, if you have a great job and make a lot of money, you'll probably stick your chest out and spout off this information with pride.

But we're called human beings, not human doings. Your identity as a person isn't wrapped up in what you do but in who God created you to be. And according to the Bible, we were created in God's image and likeness, which means God designed us to be His visual representations on the earth. We're all powerful and important simply because of who made us. You can lift your head with pride because you possess a God-like potential and enormous power. You may not know it yet, but you do. You were created by God to be just like Him and were endowed by Him with limitless potential. You're never a waste of space or an accident. You possess the ability to change the world, have the power of life and death in your tongue and have creative ability. You're not just some person who sits in a cubicle and stares at a computer screen for several hours or someone who does hair or slaves away in front of a hot stove. You're a magnificent and mighty specimen created in the image of the most powerful being in the universe, and you possess the ability to operate just like Him in this world. Think about that!

Are you selling yourself cheap by simply identifying yourself by your nine-to-five? Can your worth really be defined by an hourly wage, especially when considering what I just said about you? You can either embrace who you are and demand God's best for your life and strive to reach the stars or settle with where you are and accept the value placed on you by someone else—and that value might say that you're only worth $15 an hour. That's all!

When you know who you are, money can't define you. A car can't define you, nor can a job or career. Status can't define you. You're defined by the limitless potential God placed inside you, not the material things you possess and the opinions of others.

Furthermore, if you define yourself according to your material possessions, what will happen to you should you lose these things? What if you lose that job? What if you lose that career? What if you lose all of your money? What if your business and your house get burned down in a fire along with everything you own? You have to realize that these things never define you. They were artificial things; you're the real deal, the authentic, the one with limitless creativity and power. Not only can you rebuild, but you can build back better.

You are not simply a wife or a mother; you're so much more than that. Think about it this way: What would you be if you didn't have a man or any kids? Who would you be? You might be married today, but step back for a moment and ask yourself, "Who am I?" If you feel like you're not a whole person without your partner or you have no significance without your kids, then you need to consider what I'm saying because you're lost. Boyfriends and husbands can leave us. They can fall out of love with us and run off with another. They can even get killed in accidents, in the line of

CHAPTER 4: WHO ARE YOU, REALLY?

duty, on battlefields, or be random victims of senseless violence. So should you lose your partner, would you feel lost as if you have no sense of direction in life? And concerning children, they will leave you. They're in your life for a certain number of years only. By the time they become teenagers, they'll no longer want to hang out with you—they'll be focused on their own lives. Pretty soon, they'll be off to college, and then they'll get married and move on with their lives, leaving you with an empty nest. So if you're living for your kids only, what will you do once they're gone?

Lastly, and this might be a touchy one for some, you're not who or what your parents say you are. That is a big one because we naturally gain a sense of identity from our parents. As children, we automatically view our parents and guardians as superheroes, sometimes believing they can do no wrong. But, as kids, we don't realize our parents and guardians are flawed individuals too who lack, in many cases, the insight and wisdom to raise us the perfect way. So when our parents curse us out, we internalize their words and beat ourselves down as if we're the problem. When they neglect us, we question our value and worth and consider ourselves not good enough. When they touch us inappropriately, we view ourselves as guilty and dirty and feel undeserving of respect. But like we discussed in an earlier chapter, you must remember who truly made you: God. You are His workmanship, knitted together by Him in your mother's womb and created for a purpose.

It may take some time to clear out the negative messages in your head that you developed over time due to your upbringing. Trust me; I know the feeling. Just because you're not in that home anymore, that doesn't mean you're not still

WHO'S SLEEPING WITH YOUR HUSBAND?

affected by the things that were said and went on there. But if you do what the Bible says and "cast down every thought and imagination" that the enemy sends to keep you living in shame and then remind yourself daily of who God says you are, you will begin to cast off the chains of the past and move forward with your life.

*

The first question you must ask yourself is, "Who am I?" And we answered that question earlier. You are not your job, your title or even the labels placed on you by family, friends, loved ones and society. You are a human being created in the image of the all-powerful God. You bear His nature. The one thing you need to do is study what the Bible says about God to get a better understanding of who you are. And I can tell you now that God is a God of joy, peace, wisdom, love, creative power, great authority, beauty, confidence, wealth, resources and incredible glory, and God created you to be just like Him. He even said this about you in Psalms 8:4-8:

> "What are mere mortals that you should think about them, human beings that you should care for them? Yet you made them only a little lower than God and crowned them with glory and honor. You gave them charge of everything you made, putting all things under their authority—the flocks and the herds and all the wild animals, the birds in the sky, the fish in the sea, and everything that swims the ocean currents." (NLT)

You wear a crown of glory and honor, and were created to

CHAPTER 4: WHO ARE YOU, REALLY?

be in charge of this earth. God endowed you with divine authority over every living thing that creeps upon the face of the planet. He designed you to rule just like Him, not be dominated by life and circumstances. I mean, come on! Get a glimpse of who you really are!

If you're suffering from depression, know that depression is not a part of your nature because your nature is to be like God, who continually walks in peace, joy and power. If you're wrestling with fear and insecurity, then know that these things aren't a part of who you are because your nature was designed to operate with extreme confidence and authority like the Queen you are.

But let's go a little deeper. On a more intimate level, God made you unique; this means you have specific likes and dislikes, preferences and longings that others might not have. In addition, God has placed within you certain passions designed to propel your life toward your purpose. And that leads us to our next big question you must ask yourself, which is this:

WHAT IS MY PURPOSE?

You exist for a reason. You're not here by accident. It doesn't matter what went on with your parents; you were placed here on this earth by design. According to Esther 4:14, there was a timing for your birth. Now the enemy doesn't want you to realize this. He wants you to remain ignorant of the plans and purpose of God for your life and walk in darkness so he can manipulate your steps and lead you into destruction. The enemy wants you to turn your back on God rather than seek God for His plan for your life. That is why Satan whispers into the ears of so many people and causes them

WHO'S SLEEPING WITH YOUR HUSBAND?

to become angry and resentful towards God when tragedies strike and things don't go their way. He wants us to turn away from God, who is our help and the source of our identity, strength and purpose in life. But don't fall for the bait. God is not responsible for all of the chaos in this world. He didn't cause sin and death to enter the world; humankind did. According to Genesis chapter three, Adam and Eve brought sin and death into this world through their act of disobedience. Furthermore, the one who was pulling man's strings like a puppet, manipulating him the entire time, was Satan. God sent Jesus into this world to "bring Good News to the poor… proclaim that captives will be released… [cause] the blind [to] see, [ensure] that the oppressed will be set free, [and proclaim] that the time of the LORD's favor has come" (Luke 4:18-19, NLT). Satan, on the other hand, has one agenda, which is to "kill, steal and destroy" (John 10:10).

Yes, there is death and destruction in our world today. Yes, our world is filled with pain and suffering. But did you know God sent you to be the solution to these problems? God wants to use you to be His hands and feet, bringing healing and deliverance to those who are oppressed and bound in this world. He wants to use your tongue to edify those who feel torn down and hopeless. God wants to make a difference in this world through you. He wants to send you to every corner of the globe to make an impact in the lives of others for His name's sake. He wants to bless you so that you can help others. He wants to take your pain and suffering and use it as a testimony and tool that is used to reach others who're suffering.

In this crazy world which is experiencing Hell due to Satan and his demons' activities, some people are allowing

CHAPTER 4: WHO ARE YOU, REALLY?

themselves to be vessels of God. They bring light to the darkness, healing to the brokenhearted, hope to the hopeless, aid those in need, and the love of God to every person who feels like God has abandoned them. We see this when we witness people rally together behind the worst catastrophes, sacrificing to help others and the charitable work of churches and humanitarian organizations.

Your purpose is so much bigger than you. God placed certain gifts, talents and passions in your heart so that you can serve those who're in that arena and improve their quality of living while turning their eyes back to the Creator. You were given that artistic ability for a reason. God gave you that singing voice for a reason. You have the mind of an engineer for a reason. You desire to be a doctor or a lawyer for a reason. Don't just use your gift; use it for the glory of God; use it to lead men and women back to God. Our ultimate purpose in life is to use what God has given us to lead men and women back to Himself and bring glory to His name.

Now, the question becomes, what has God given you to use in this world? What's your gift, your passion? Your passion is that which you'd do for free. What's yours? And keep in mind that, in life, our passions do change. We do enter into different seasons of our lives where our focuses shift. For example, you might be in a season in your life where your focus is on your kids. Still, God may later place it in your heart to go back to school to get that degree in Business Administration or Counseling, or you might find yourself revisiting that old dream of owning several salons or opening a restaurant. You might even discover a call of ministry in your life. I was shocked when I learned that God called me to be a minister, public speaker or author. I didn't see myself doing these things when I was a little girl.

The way to discover your purpose is to go to the one who created you—God—and spend time with Him. The more you pray and seek His face, the more He will reveal to you your purpose and the hidden gifts and abilities that He placed inside of you. The Bible says, "For God is working in you, giving you the desire and the power to do what pleases him" (Philippians 2:13, NLT). It also says in Psalm 37:4, "Take delight in the LORD, and he will give you your heart's desires" (NLT). When the Bible says God will give you your heart's desires, it means God will place His desires in your heart and cause them to come to pass. So the moral of the story is the more time you spend with God in prayer and meditation, pursuing after Him, the more He'll unveil your life's purpose to you. But you have to seek Him for that understanding.

MORE DISCOVERY

You are worth the investment of time and energy. You can make no greater investment than to take the time to get to know yourself. And you need to learn who you are on a microscopic level. What makes you unique? What makes you tick? Have you taken the time to discover your needs as a woman? How do you want to be loved? Do you want a man to send you roses and chocolates constantly? Do you prefer to be held, caressed, or touched? Or do you value compliments—words of affirmation—above all else? How do you want your partner to love you? You can't communicate this to your partner if you don't know it.

Do you take time out for yourself during the day and throughout the week? If so, what do you like to do? Go for

CHAPTER 4: WHO ARE YOU, REALLY?

walks? Exercise? Go dancing? To the movies? Read? Write? Visit loved ones and friends? Travel? Go hiking? Do other adventurous stuff like white water rafting or spelunking? I'm not asking you what you enjoy doing for others. I'm asking you what you enjoy doing for yourself. That isn't selfish thinking; it's self-care.

It's time you carve out time for yourself and focus on the things that make you happy. If you fail to do this, you may wake up one day feeling resentful towards those around you without knowing why. I'll tell you why—you feel smothered by them as if they won't allow you to live your life, rob you of personal happiness and satisfaction while forcing you to serve their needs only. But they're not responsible for your happiness; you are. It's your job to get in touch with your true self, study yourself, discover yourself, answer the questions I posed at the beginning of this chapter and seek God for His divine purpose in your life. People will treat you like a servant and a slave if you allow them to, and you'll only allow yourself to be treated like this if you lack an understanding of who you are and why you're here. And even when it comes to serving others, you will serve them for the wrong reason if you don't know who you are. You will serve others to receive their validation and approval rather than serving them from a place of genuine love and selfless sacrifice. You will be kind to others only so they can be kind to you in return rather than being kind to others without needing and expecting anything from them. That was me! I am a giver; I give and give until it hurts. Giving is one of my spiritual gifts. I LOVE TO GIVE. But sometimes it becomes too much because those around you will see it as normal for you to continue giving to them and not notice that you have needs too. Now is a great time to take inventory of what makes you happy and Start implementing it. The time is always NOW!

REDISCOVER who you are and Truly Live Free to be You!

Chapter 5
Taking Care Of You

As discussed in the previous chapter, we need to take the time to get to know ourselves. I don't care how busy you are, stop and take some "me-time". If you don't, you will become burned out; when you're burned out and exhausted, you won't be any good to anyone else. Self-care is needed before you try to take care of everyone else in your life. When you need a break, take it. Listen to your body; it will tell you when you're going overboard and when you're doing too much. When your body says stop, stop. When your body says it's done, quit. Don't worry if another person doesn't like it. You have to value how you feel and be true to yourself, remembering that you are responsible for yourself.

It took me a while to learn what I'm about to share with you here, but it was worth the trip. I had to learn what self-care was because I'd been neglecting myself for so long to focus on others. And sadly, the more I neglected myself for others, the more resentful I became towards them. And the crazy thing is, it wasn't their fault I was doing this. I was hurting myself because I'd never taken the time to heal from my past wounds. I was a people-pleaser seeking outside validation and acceptance because of the festering wounds in my soul. Since I never felt good enough as a girl, I looked for people to make me think I was good enough in their eyes. I'd work overtime just for their approval at the expense of losing myself and denying myself. That wasn't someone else's fault; it was mine. I didn't love and value myself. I didn't have the right opinion of myself, nor did I see the need to affirm myself. So I left that up to others when it was always my job.

For so long, I allowed others to make me depressed. I hung on their every opinion of me as if my life depended on it. I would feel ashamed if I upset certain people like I did something wrong. It didn't matter if I didn't want to do something because it made me uncomfortable; my first question was always, "How do they feel about what I did?"

Finally, I began to understand that my obsession with other people's thoughts and feelings was a detriment in my life. So the first person I needed to consider when making a decision was Jeri (me). She was, and is, my greatest responsibility and the only one whose thoughts, emotions, and actions I can control. So after taking some time to discover who I was, I began researching ways to practice self-care. Here are a few tips I found:

SELF-CARE TIPS

According to Psychology Today, there are several steps you

CHAPTER 5: TAKING CARE OF YOU

must take to take care of yourself. These steps include giving your body adequate rest (sleep), eating healthy, exercising, practicing the art of saying no, pampering yourself, doing something you enjoy every day, enjoying the sunlight, unplugging from all of the gadgets and devices, and affirming yourself. Let's examine each of these.

GETTING ADEQUATE REST

Most people can't rest at night because of anxiety. Anxiety is caused by thinking too much and too hard about circumstances that are beyond your control. For example, let's say you work in a highly stressful environment. Your job is very demanding. You have a million things to do. You'll probably find yourself freaking out due to the load of responsibility on your back and will freak out the closer deadlines approach, fearing missing one. In these cases, people tend to overwork themselves to accommodate others. As a result, they'll stretch themselves too thin. In many cases, they will take on more than they can chew.

In America today, more people are overworked and dying from stress-related illnesses than in any other country. More people are on antidepressants and medications for anxiety in this country than anywhere else. We're working ourselves to death. We need pills to go to bed, several cups of coffee to stay awake when up, five-hour energy to keep going after we've gulped down several cups of coffee to keep going, and then we need pills to help us unwind and go to sleep. We're destroying our bodies and our minds. We live in a fight-or-flight state, overstimulated by the nonstop flow of news and information from television and social media. We take our phones with us to bed, check our emails and social media pages, and respond to texts and calls long after we've clocked out. When do we ever rest?

Some entrepreneurs may brag that they can't afford to take vacations. So they slave away in their companies, exchanging one full-time job for another, working over fifty and sixty-hour workweeks. They work all week and then play catchup on weekends, trying to complete projects they couldn't get to during the week. And the whole time they're working themselves to death, their kids are slipping into sex, drugs and gangs, their spouses bear the weight of marital neglect, and they're still sinking deeper and deeper.

You must learn to recognize and be comfortable with your limitations. You're not omnipresent—you can't be everywhere at one time. And although God created you in His image and likeness, you are not God, which means that as long as you're in this body, you still have a few limitations. You can't fly like a bird, live underwater like a fish, run faster than a speeding bullet, and you can't solve everyone's problems and make everyone happy. You have limitations; embrace them. Tell people upfront what you can and cannot do, how much you'll be willing to take on and where your limits are. Draw a line in the sand early by being selective of what you will and will not do, what you can and cannot handle, and how much you're willing to do.

Set boundaries around yourself and control your time and energy. Don't overload yourself to prove a point to someone else. Don't even overload yourself just for money. If someone gets upset with you because you can't meet all of their demands, be content with them being upset. Just don't kill yourself to make others like you. If you lose money, you can get it back; if you lose a client, realize there will be oth-

CHAPTER 5: TAKING CARE OF YOU

ers up the road; and if you lose a job, realize there are other jobs available. If one person dislikes you, don't start disliking yourself. Trust me; you'll be just fine. It's not the end of the world. Tomorrow contains plenty of opportunities, but let this be a lesson to you not to take on too much and stress yourself out.

Learn to trust others with tasks rather than take on all the work yourself. Believe me when I tell you that others can do what you do and do it better than you can. They're all around you, waiting for you to call upon them. Learn to delegate and share the load with them. Place tasks in the hands of others and go and get some rest. If you don't rest, your body will shut down, and you'll have no choice but to step away from that job or project. I am still learning to walk more diligently day by day. This journey is a daily walk.

EATING HEALTHY

Your body is like a car—it needs fuel. Think of your body as a Mercedes—it requires the premium grade gasoline to run properly; it can't survive off of regular or mid-grade gas. The regular-grade gas is what we call junk food. Now, don't get me wrong. I like good hot french fries from an excellent fast food restaurant, but that shouldn't be every day. *Pray for me!* You can't live on junk food, or you will find yourself experiencing all types of health problems: high cholesterol, diabetes, malnutrition, cancer, and more. Fast foods are generally heavily processed foods with a more excellent shelf-life. That means they are filled with many chemicals designed to make these foods last longer so businesses can profit more. You already know all of this, but this is our challenge. We must do better with our eating habits. Have you noticed that organ-

WHO'S SLEEPING WITH YOUR HUSBAND?

ic foods spoil much quicker than nonorganic foods? That's because organic foods lack the chemicals that other foods possess. Organic foods are just the way God created them: natural. They're healthier for our bodies. I am striving to do better. Come, let's do this together.

Eating healthier is a way we take care of our bodies. When we value our bodies, we take care of them. You may not like this point, but our physical appearances often indicate our internal beliefs and self-perceptions. I am not talking about our weight. How much you weigh does not always indicate whether you are healthy or not. Skinny people get sick as well as overweight people. Being healthy is much more than weighing a certain amount on the scale. When we don't value ourselves, we let ourselves go down. We can sometimes eat junk and destroy our health because we don't feel good about ourselves. There's a psychological component to this. If you feel unworthy of love, or you've been abused, you might cope with the feeling of shame by using food or even letting your body go down as a way of repelling people. We need to change how we feel about ourselves to reflect a positive self-image in our bodies.

When we eat right, we feel better. I know you know this already, so please use this as a reminder. The proper diet can improve our memories, help us shed unwanted pounds, and improve our moods. You'll be surprised how much of the depression and anxiety we feel is caused by copious amounts of sugar and caffeine. We can improve our mood and increase our lifespan by cutting back on certain foods.

EXERCISE
Oh boy...this is my weak spot, but I am determined to get on

CHAPTER 5: TAKING CARE OF YOU

the right track with exercising and stay there! Not to repeat what you've undoubtedly heard others say repeatedly, but we must exercise if we're going to take care of our bodies. Like cars, our bodies were designed to move. These are some of the benefits of moving your body:

- Improves memory and brain function
- Protect against chronic diseases
- Sheds unwanted pounds
- Lowers blood pressure and improves heart health
- Improve the quality of your sleep
- Reduce feelings of anxiety and depression
- Increases your energy
- Improves your sex life
- and more

Some companies have observed that employees who exercise routinely perform better in their jobs, and because of this observation, they provide free gym memberships to their employees. I'll admit that I don't get up in the mornings excited about working out, but I understand the importance of exercise, and *whew...* don't mention drinking enough water. I don't know if you struggle as I do with drinking enough water, but that's a big one for me. I have to have something with some flavor to it. However, by becoming conscious of these habits, I've made a turn in the right direction, and I pray you'll join me in this one too. Come on! We can do this together!

PRACTICING THE ART OF SAYING NO
This goes back to my earlier point of not taking on too

much. You have to learn to say no. When someone attempts to place more on you than you can handle, kindly and politely let them know you cannot accommodate all of their demands and don't feel ashamed of turning down that which you cannot handle.

When I think of this, I think about the movie "The Devil Wears Prada" starring Meryl Streep and Anne Hathaway. Meryl's character, Miranda Priestly, was an obnoxious and overbearing boss who gave her assistant, Andrea (Anne Hathaway), impossible demands. For example, she wanted Andrea to book her a flight to get home despite all flights being canceled, get a copy of the newest "Harry Potter" book for her daughters before the book was even released, and more. Poor Andrea sacrificed time with her family and friends to accomplish the tasks she'd been given. And in the end, Andrea realized that the job wasn't worth it. She realized that she had nearly lost her boyfriend and was throwing other meaningful relationships down the drain to meet the demands of a woman who was impossible to please. She discovered when it was nearly too late that she should have said no a million times to the things her boss was asking her to do. She shouldn't have canceled her dinner date with her father to accommodate her boss. She shouldn't have skipped out on her boyfriend's birthday celebration to accommodate her boss. She shouldn't have sought to live up to standards that were impossible to live up to. She should have said no.

You have God's permission to say no. If it doesn't feel right to you or will cost you something too valuable to give up, provide an astounding "no" to whoever is asking you to do it. If it's going to cost you your self-esteem or cause you to compromise your integrity, principles and values, shout

CHAPTER 5: TAKING CARE OF YOU

no from the rooftop. Most of all, if what someone is asking you to do will cause you to walk contrary to God's Word and will, scream no. Practice saying no until you become a pro.

Pampering Yourself
This is simple. Take some time out for yourself and treat yourself. When I say treat yourself, take yourself to someplace nice, whether a spa, a restaurant, a movie, or some other place you've wanted to visit, and then reward yourself. Get the spa treatment. Get the full package: the massage, the facial, the manicure and pedicure, etc. Order what you want at the restaurant. Enjoy that movie. Shop to you drop but don't spend all your money. Allow the cares of this world to slip to the back-burner and remind yourself that everyone else and everything else can wait until you're done.

Do Something You Enjoy Everyday
Again, find out what you enjoy doing and do it. Do you enjoy reading? Well, find a good book and immerse yourself in its world. Do you enjoy dancing, skating, bowling, drawing, painting, hiking, taking long walks, going to the gym, writing, or cooking? If you enjoy these things, do them. Make it a point to do them. Set an appointment with yourself daily by scheduling a time to do them. And don't miss your appointment.

Get Some Sunlight
You must step outside and get some sunlight and some fresh air. Of the benefits of sunlight, I want to mention a few: sunlight produces vitamin D, fights depression, reduces stress, improves sleep, and improves your immune system. Sunlight

increases serotonin levels in the body, which fights depression. Vitamin D is instrumental in fighting off diseases in the body and improving our physical health. That's why you must take breaks throughout the day and step outside to stand in the sun, especially when dealing with a highly stressful job or environment.

Unplug From The Gadgets And Devices

We have to let our minds rest. To do this, we must unplug social media and lay our smartphones aside. If you're connected to social media and constantly stimulating your brain with a constant flow of information, news and propaganda, you aren't allowing your brain to recharge. You aren't letting your brain rest; this is the fastest way to get burned out.

You have to clock out; this doesn't simply mean punching out at the job, but it also means permanently ending your work day. Anything left undone at the end of the day will receive immediate attention the following day. Any tasks that didn't get done today will get done tomorrow. Any calls you didn't make today, make them tomorrow. For any texts or calls that come in after hours, feel free to put the phone on vibrate or silent and avoid answering them. Only if it's a serious emergency should you entertain work-related matters after hours. If you are an entrepreneur, you set your work hours and don't let people stress you. Some people act like everything is an emergency. Don't give those types of people your peace of mind.

Unplug your devices, tune in to your partner and family, and do something just for you. Shift your focus now to that which is most important in your life. Ask your loved ones about their day and do something fun with them. En-

CHAPTER 5: TAKING CARE OF YOU

joy a good movie, discussion, or board game. Whatever you do, unplug and unwind.

Affirm Yourself

This is perhaps the most crucial step in self-care. Experts explain that throughout the day, we think around eighty-thousand thoughts, and over 80% of them are negative. That means we usually put ourselves down all day long by speaking negatively about ourselves; that's a horrible habit. And to make matters worse, we're constantly exposed to negative criticism of us from other people. It might be a boss or a coworker. It might be a loved one, a family member or a spouse. It might be a stranger on the street who's having a bad day and want to take their frustrations out on someone else. It might be a client, customer, church member, or leader. There's always someone with something negative to say about you; their words can damage your self-esteem and self-image.

You might perceive yourself as a failure if someone calls you a failure. If someone says you're ugly, you might perceive yourself as ugly. And depending on who says these things, those words will affect us more. Furthermore, if you grew up believing you're ugly, the second someone calls you ugly, you will take that as a confirmation that you're ugly. In other words, their negative criticism of you will only confirm what you already believe about yourself. That is why so many people stay defeated in their minds—their minds are on a constant loop of negative, critical words.

The Bible says, "For as he thinketh in his heart, so is he" (Proverbs 23:7). If you continue to think of yourself as a failure, you'll act like a failure. If you think of yourself as inadequate, you'll begin to behave inadequately. The way you carry yourself is determined by what you say to yourself. Your words create the programming that your subconscious mind operates on. For example, if you subconsciously believe you're unlovable and undesirable, then you'll sabotage relationships by doing things to drive people away.

The key is to change your subconscious programming by changing your thoughts. To do this, you must first change your words. Change what you say about yourself and stop agreeing with other people's negative criticism. To do this, you need to identify your strengths, accomplishments, successes, wins, positive attributes, positive values and principles, and the wonderful plans God has for your life, and then you need to say them out loud. Whenever a negative thought pops up in your mind about yourself, remind yourself of the truth about yourself by stating the positive things I just mentioned. Quit lying to yourself by exaggerating your mistakes and making it seem like you're always messing up because you're not. You have more wins than losses, successes than failures, and more positive attributes than shortcomings. And even your shortcomings aren't something to get hung up over since everyone has them—that means you're no better and no worse than others. So they can't judge you when they're no different from you.

Speak positive affirmations over yourself daily; do this first thing in the morning. Once you make this a habit, you'll find your attitude towards yourself and towards your life starting to change. You will begin to look for the positive in life rather than always expecting the worse. Most of all, you will begin to change your subconscious programming and attract the right things in life.

Chapter 6
Sex In The City

LADIES, HOW'S YOUR SEX LIFE? ARE YOU BEING fulfilled sexually the way you dreamed you would be? Then, it's time to regain your sexual prowess. Like Stella, it's time to get your groove back. It's time to become the fierce lioness you were meant to be in the boardroom and the bedroom, and this is only accomplished by regaining the confidence you may have lost somewhere along the way.

God wants you to be a lioness. I'm not talking about the animal. When I talk about a lioness, I'm referring to a woman who exists in all her glory. She's courageous and empowered and ready to rock the world. She is fearless and bold. But, she's also aware of her responsibilities and takes care of business. I'm talking about a woman who knows what she wants and isn't afraid to go after it. This woman isn't afraid to be in charge and is not afraid to be on top of her game.

WHO'S SLEEPING WITH YOUR HUSBAND?

GIRL, LET'S TALK ABOUT SEX!

You deserve pleasure. I know that may sound strange, but it's true. God wants us to enjoy sex; that's why He created it. The only caveat is that God designed sex to be experienced in marriage.

Sex isn't merely a religious duty; it's an activity designed to bring two individuals together in a greater, more intimate way. The Bible says, "The two will become one flesh" (Mark 10:7-8, NIV). That's where the concept of soul-ties come from. When two or more people engage in sex, their spirits become one; they connect not only physically but spiritually. That's why Paul wrote, "And don't you realize that if a man joins himself to a prostitute, he becomes one body with her? For the Scriptures say, 'The two are united into one'" (1 Corinthians 6:16, NLT). Who would want to become one with someone full of soul-ties with other people? You don't know what type of spirits you allow to enter your body when having sex with random people, especially those with a promiscuous lifestyle.

At one point, I was that girl who was lost and confused. I didn't know who I was, and I thought low of myself and allowed men to tell me who I was while leading me in the wrong direction. In light of the things I let happen in my life, I thank God that He saved me from destruction. God's Grace kept me while I was stuck on stupid, doing things backwards. In the upcoming years, after I started to discover the truth, I repented and asked God to break every soul-tie I had developed.

Sometimes, we can't understand why, even after breaking up with someone, we can't seem to shake the con-

CHAPTER 6: SEX IN THE CITY

nection with that person. It seems like that person is still with us, inside us, a part of our lives, although they're physically separate. We even find ourselves craving them despite knowing they're bad for business and making our intentions to leave them alone clear. And yet, they keep appearing in our dreams at night; the sensation of their touch still haunts our sensory memory. That is because their spirits are still intertwined with ours. It takes God's power to break these bonds and restore us to a state of purity and wholeness.

As you walk your life journey, to be free of those bondages, soul ties and chains, you must acknowledge and ask for guidance and forgiveness. Forgive yourself and be set free! Free to live on your terms and your way!

Going back to my earlier point, sex is something God created for our pleasure. He designed sex so husbands and wives could enjoy each other, meet a deep physical need for connection, and keep the human race going. He loves to see us bonding in intimate ways. The Bible contains an entire book that deals with sexual intimacy and foreplay; it's called Solomon's Song of Songs (or the Songs of Solomon). Within this book, you find verses like these:

> "My beloved thrust his hand through the latch-opening; my heart began to pound for him." (5:4-5, NIV)

> "Your navel is perfectly formed like a goblet filled with mixed wine. Between your thighs lies a mound of wheat bordered with lilies. Your breasts are like two fawns, twin fawns of a gazelle." (7:2-3, NLT)

WHO'S SLEEPING WITH YOUR HUSBAND?

> "I said, 'I will climb the palm tree; I will take hold of its fruit.' May your breasts be like clusters of grapes on the vine, the fragrance of your breath like apples, and your mouth like the best wine. She: May the wine go straight to my beloved, flowing gently over lips and teeth." (7:8-9, NIV)

And Solomon also left some steamy content in his other books:

> "May your fountain be blessed, and may you rejoice in the wife of your youth. A loving doe, a graceful deer— may her breasts satisfy you always, may you ever be intoxicated with her love." (Proverbs 5:18-19, NIV)

This sounds nothing like a boring and dull God or a God who detests sex as dirty. On the contrary, several passages in the Bible show us just how sexy God's people are. God's ideal husband for you talks to you the way Solomon talked to his wife. He brags about you and sends you text messages describing how beautiful you are to him throughout the day; he also knows every inch of and curve of your body and how he wants to gently kiss every part of you once he gets home from work. He sends you flowers at home or while you're at your job, showers you with gifts to say, "I love you," and serenades you with romance. This man is faithful to you; he's selfless like Christ when it comes to you, loving you the way Christ loves His bride, the church.

In less romantic terms, Paul addressed God's desire for sexual intimacy between couples in 1 Corinthians 7:2-5:

CHAPTER 6: SEX IN THE CITY

> "But because there is so much sexual immorality, each man should have his own wife, and each woman should have her own husband. The husband should fulfill his wife's sexual needs, and the wife should fulfill her husband's needs. The wife gives authority over her body to her husband, and the husband gives authority over his body to his wife. Do not deprive each other of sexual relations, unless you both agree to refrain from sexual intimacy for a limited time so you can give yourselves more completely to prayer. Afterward, you should come together again so that Satan won't be able to tempt you because of your lack of self-control." (NLT)

To put it bluntly, God is concerned about your sexual and emotional needs. He wants you to have these needs met. Believe it or not, your physical and emotional needs are high on His list. He didn't intend for you to live life alone, starving for intimacy. So He created marriage to meet those needs.

An article entitled "Faith is the new aphrodisiac: 'Highly religious' couples have better sex lives than their secular counterparts, survey reveals" says,

> "Some 38 percent of married women and 33 percent of married men in 'highly religious' relationships say they strongly agree that they are satisfied with the sexual relationship they have with their partner, according to the survey of U.S. adults by the right-leaning Institute for Family Studies. That's significantly higher than the 23 percent of women

and 20 percent of men in secular marriages who feel the same way. It also surpasses the satisfaction of men (28 percent) and women (22 percent) who are in less religious or mixed-religion marriages." (www.DailyMail.co.uk)

Sex done God's way, is way better than what the world is reporting. Sex in the context of marriage, with God at the center, is reportedly much better, healthier and more frequent than sex in the secular arena. When done the right way, sex is more meaningful because it is focused on serving rather than selfishly taking. When lust and selfishness are the driving forces behind our actions, they only leave us feeling empty in the end. Sex becomes meaningless because there is no real devotion, security and genuine connection. You don't even know if that person will be beside you in the bed come morning.

BACK ON TOP

Now that you know God wants you to be happy sexually let's discover how we can reclaim this happiness. First, you must recover your sense of identity in this area. If you've been the victim of sexual abuse, then take the time to get professional help to overcome the trauma of that experience. Sexual abuse, rape and molestation hammer a person's self-image, making them feel ashamed or undeserving of respect. Remember: shame doesn't say you have a problem; it says you are the problem. Therefore, you must realize you are not the problem and that you can reclaim ownership over your body.

Another form of abuse is being compared to other women, especially the ones found in porn movies. Yes, por-

CHAPTER 6: SEX IN THE CITY

nography has a damaging effect on a woman's psyche—and men's. Porn twists one's perception of reality and causes a chemical dependency on perverted acts and sexualized violence, as revealed by science. Each time a person watches porn, they rewire their brains only to derive a sense of pleasure from a certain type of image and cause a release of the pleasure hormone dopamine in the brain. That leads to pornography addiction, where people can't get aroused unless they're looking at pornography, imagining it, or forcing their partner to imitate what they saw on their computer or television screen.

As a woman, when your partner compares your body to another woman's and expects you to outdo an actress who gets paid to practice and perform sexual acts as a job, that can be humiliating; it can cause insecurity and the feeling of worthlessness. Truthfully, you'll never be able to compete with an actress. She's an actress! Everything she does is an act, a performance, a front for the camera. There's nothing real about it! That's like comparing your man to a hyper-romantic, flawless character from a romance novel. These are unrealistic expectations; it's like comparing your body to that found on the cover of a beauty magazine where the cover girl has been edited and airbrushed to perfection.

Stop shaming yourself and comparing yourself to fictional characters. Instead, embrace every part of your body. Embrace your stretch marks, birthmarks, wrinkles, moles, bumps and every other blemish. "We all have them!" Stop being ashamed of your body. The man God has for you will love you and all your imperfections, realizing he has plenty of flaws. Our bodies change over time, and there's not much we can do about that. Yes, fix yourself up and take good care

85

of yourself, but don't obsess over perfection because that's an unattainable goal. Give yourself some grace.

*

Believe it or not, confident men love confident women. They love women who aren't scared to use what their mothers gave them. Knowing who she is and what she has, her confidence will resonate strongly in the bedroom and make the sexual experience more exciting. When she operates with this type of confidence, she'll do several things:

BE ADVENTUROUS IN THE BEDROOM

When you think about what drew your husband to you, it was the fun-loving, adventurous attitude you had. He fell in love with the girl who had a zest for life and didn't mind exploring new and exciting things. No one wants to stay stuck in a boring, mundane routine, yet that can easily happen once we get married and settle down. We stop being fun, unpredictable and a little bit crazy. We become tame, perhaps a little too tame. We stop looking for new ways to please each other. We start to believe we don't have to work to win our partners over because we already have them. That's the wrong attitude to have of both partners.

Put the fun and spontaneity back into your sex life. Try different positions. Try having sex in other places, like renting a hotel or visiting an exotic location. Change the scenery, buy new lingerie or a new outfit, practice things like talking dirty during sex, and flirt more. Send your man exotic pictures while he's at work with sexy messages (commonly called "sexting"). Find out what he likes and fulfill that fantasy, not just for him but for you.

CHAPTER 6: SEX IN THE CITY

And speaking of fantasies...

TALK ABOUT FETISHES, DESIRES AND FANTASIES

Sexually confident women aren't afraid to go there. They don't feel insecure, so they are willing and open to trying different things. They know that's a part of the game, the tool to spice up the bedroom. That isn't the same as comparing yourself to another woman because the sexually confident woman is clear on what she will and will not do. She keeps her standards intact and not going where she isn't comfortable in the bedroom.

The mere fact that his woman is confident and secure enough within herself to strike up the conversation about sexual fantasies is a turn-on for a man. He feels comfortable around her, not fearing that mentioning his innermost longings will send her into a coma. But, of course, that's taking into account the idea that such fantasies are rooted in reality. They are within the realm of that which is reasonable and morally acceptable to what you want.

Providing a safe, judgment-free zone where personal expression is allowed creates a more intimate environment, which leads to a closer relationship.

INITIATE SEX

Confident women don't depend on their partners for their sexual freedom. She permits herself to be open about what she wants and needs. She's not one to suffer in silence and bite her tongue regarding her needs. She knows marriage is a 50/50 arrangement where both parties are obligated to serve each other.

WHO'S SLEEPING WITH YOUR HUSBAND?

COMMUNICATE HER SEXUAL DESIRES

The sexually confident woman tells her man what she wants him to do to her. This might not be very comforting, but many men are clueless about what women want. Instead, tell him where and how you want to be touched and what you want him to do. Be open and communicate as he may worry that he is doing the wrong thing may kill the mood, so he relies on his woman's guidance and vice-versa.

Sex is a learning experience, so having only one partner is important. You might spend years just getting to know their body, discovering where their erogenous zones are and what turns them on. And what may work for one might not work for another. Therefore, learning about your partner's body will only cause the sex to flow even smoother and make the experience even more enjoyable. That way, as a sexually confident woman, you can focus more on...

TAKING RESPONSIBILITY FOR HER SEXUAL PLEASURE

Your sensual pleasure doesn't begin with your man; it starts with you. When you're the lioness, you pursue sexual pleasure rather than wait for it to happen to you. You become more of the aggressor. You know your body and what it wants and needs, and you seek enjoyment during the sexual experience. You allow yourself to feel everything you've been waiting to feel, not holding back, not denying your body what it deserves. You don't see sex as a task but as a path to ecstasy and euphoria. You learn to enjoy sex rather than loathe it. This newfound attitude not only gives you the satisfaction you crave, but it also gives your man the satisfaction he craves.

CHAPTER 6: SEX IN THE CITY

He gains a sense of pleasure from feeling like he "nailed it" in the bedroom—and by "nailed it," I meant he gave you the greatest, most intense pleasure.

You might ask, "Why is this chapter so important?" It is important because it enables you to be truly free. Sex is a big part of your marriage that most people don't want to talk about. Some women believe you should leave it up to your husband to fulfill your desires and dreams and create the atmosphere. I challenge you to co-partner with your husband and create a mood, space, and atmosphere. Know that what's important to you is valuable and needed.

You have what it takes to be that lioness in the Boardroom and the Bedroom. It's time to make your fantasies come true because you, my dear, are the woman who is sleeping with your husband!

Rediscover your passion! It would be best if you were healthy and whole. It is time you pick up the pieces of your life and create the life you only dreamed of.

Never give the pieces of your life's satisfaction and growth to someone else to manage. You only get one life. It's time you live it!

WHO'S SLEEPING WITH YOUR HUSBAND?

PRAYER FOR BREAKING SOUL-TIES:

Dear Heavenly Father, I thank you for sending your Son Jesus the Christ to save my soul and set me free from every bondage and entanglement. Today, I repent for the sins I committed and surrender my body to you. Holy Spirit, I thank you that your power has broken the power of sin off my life and that the blood of Jesus has washed away my sins. Today, I am a brand new creation in Christ Jesus.

Lord, I thank you for redeeming me from every curse and severing every soul-tie in my life. You have broken every covenant with men I have established, and I am now free. My body is now the property of the Holy Spirit. I am no longer under the power and influence of any power of force other than God's.

I thank you that it is already done. In Jesus' name, I pray, amen.

Chapter 7
Live Your Life

OKAY. YOU DISCOVERED FROM CHAPTER ONE THAT you're here for a purpose, and that's why life hasn't broken you. You discovered from chapter two that your past doesn't define you and that you can set a new precedent in your life and break cycles of destructive behaviors. You discovered from chapter three how to secure your heart and heal from bitterness while setting fair expectations of others and yourself. You discovered your true worth and significance in chapter four, learning that your identity as a person isn't defined by what you do and what you have but by the incredible creative power you possess and the purpose of God that rests upon your life. You discovered in chapter five how to value yourself and prioritize your needs in life. And you just learned how to reclaim power over your sexuality in our previous chapter. Now, it's time to take all that you've

WHO'S SLEEPING WITH YOUR HUSBAND?

learned and live your life. It's time for you to go forward and be that unstoppable force God created you to be. It's time for you to enter into beast mode.

*

When you look in the mirror, you should see a different woman. Sure, you have the same color and complexion, the same hair color, eye color, the same shape, the same body type, but now you have a different perspective of yourself. You realize that the woman who'd been sleeping in your bed for the last several days, weeks, months or years was an imposter. She was a twisted version of who you are, a clone that lacks everything that makes you who you are. But now, that woman is dead. She's gone. There's only you—the real you. So let's get back to her assignment in life. Let's pick back up with what she needs to do moving forward. To do this, we're going to revisit a few things and then set some realistic goals. Let's get started.

DREAM AGAIN

The first thing I want you to do is dream again. Permit yourself to explore the furthest reaches of your potential in your mind. Too many adults perceive dreams and imagination as a tool to keep children preoccupied, but that's not the case. God gave you imagination for a reason, and He intends for you to use it. Every great invention began with someone's imagination. Thomas Edison imagined the lightbulb before he created it. The Wright Brothers imagined themselves soaring through the air like a bird before creating the airplane. Walt Disney imagined Disney World before building the magical theme park. So let me ask you this question: What

CHAPTER 7: LIVE YOUR LIFE

was your childhood dream? Better yet, what was your dream when you became a young woman? Did you see yourself as an entrepreneur? Did you dream of holding a high-ranking office in the political arena? Did you see yourself as a professional athlete, actress, or entertainer? What was it? Heck... What is it now?

As we discussed in chapter four, passions and gifts are deeply embedded in your heart to point you toward your purpose. The Bible says, "Guard your heart above all else, for it determines the course of your life" (Proverbs 4:23, NLT). That which is inside of your heart determines what direction your life goes in. So, as you begin this new journey of faith, allow God to pour into your heart. Daily, spend time with Him so that He can impart His plans into your heart. He wants to give you a new dream and activate the power of your imagination so that you can see where He's taking you.

That's powerful! God wants you to see yourself in the place where He's taking you before you even get there. You must see yourself in your place of destiny in your mind's eye before arriving there; that's a spiritual law. You've probably heard it said, "If it's not in your mind, it will never be in your future." That revelation has been the guiding light for so many visionaries and highly accomplished people, from Oprah Winfrey to Tyler Perry. These men and women lived from the inside out, not the outside in. They created the life they wanted to live rather than accepting what life gave them. Oprah was fired from her job as an anchor, but she didn't accept what life gave her. Instead, she created her path and went into daytime television, where she amassed a fortune, building a media empire and becoming a billionaire. Tyler Perry endured homelessness while pursuing the dream

WHO'S SLEEPING WITH YOUR HUSBAND?

God placed in his heart to write and produce plays. Today, he too is a billionaire with a media empire—glad he turned down the job working for the phone company and continued to set his sights on something far greater.

Are you setting your sights on something far greater than what's before your physical eyes? If not, then let me remind you that God didn't design you to be mediocre and barely get by. God didn't design you to work a nine-to-five and go through the bland routines of everyday life. Instead, God created you to rule, dominate, have dominion on the earth, be an earthly ambassador or His divine Kingdom, and make an impact in this world. God wants you to be blessed. And as the Bible reveals, "The blessing of the LORD makes a person rich, and he adds no sorrow with it" (Proverbs 10:22, NLT).

God wants to put you in a position where you can effect change in the earth for His glory. That takes financial abundance; it also requires influence with people. But you must be daring enough to dream, to break loose from the confinement of your comfort zone and go to greater heights. Sure there will be challenges, but you have a giant-crushing, mountain-moving God on your side. There's no need to worry, to draw back in fear. Trust God to bring His plans to pass in your life.

Be daring and bold enough to ask God to do greater and mightier things in your life. The Bible tells you,

> "What is causing the quarrels and fights among you? Don't they come from the evil desires at war within you? You want what you don't have, so you scheme and kill to get it. You are jealous of what

CHAPTER 7: LIVE YOUR LIFE

others have, but you can't get it, so you fight and wage war to take it away from them. Yet you don't have what you want because you don't ask God for it." (James 4:1-2, NLT)

You haven't asked. You won't ask. Why? Because you think you're not worth it? Well, that shouldn't even be in your thinking, not now. NOT EVER! We dismissed that lie already. God created you in the image of greatness to be great. So ask for it.

That reminds me of a particular prayer in the Old Testament. It was a simple prayer but a profound one. So I want this to be your prayer:

"Oh, that you would bless me and expand my territory! Please be with me in all that I do, and keep me from all trouble and pain!" (1 Chronicles 4:10, NLT)

The exciting thing is God answered that prayer. He gave Jabez everything he asked for. And who was Jabez? Was he someone special? Was he a great prophet? Was he closer to God than any other man? No! Jabez was a simple man previously unknown and unmentioned in the Bible. The only thing he's known for is having the boldness and the audacity to ask God to make him great by enlarging his territory. Territory equates to more than just land; it also symbolizes influence. Do you possess that boldness? Sure, you do. It's already inside of you.

It's time for you to ask God to make you awesome, to take you to greater heights. It's time to receive that di-

WHO'S SLEEPING WITH YOUR HUSBAND?

vine download from Heaven—that dream, that vision from God. And after you receive it, you must implement the next step—

WRITE THE VISION

Habakkuk 2:2 says, "And the LORD answered me, and said, Write the vision, and make it plain upon tables, that he may run that readeth it." If you don't write down your vision and goals, you will never accomplish them. There's great power in recording your goals onto paper. For one, you won't forget what they are. So many people receive great ideas that they never act on, and one of the reasons for this is they don't write them down. When a goal is written, it constantly reminds you where you're going and what you're supposed to be doing; it activates the power of focus, provides direction for your life, and even tells your brain what to search for and focus on.

Furthermore, God told the prophet to write down the vision so others could see it. Every vision from God will require help from a team; however, if your goals and vision aren't clear to the team, no one will know what to do. The Bible says, "Where there is no vision, the people perish" (Proverbs 29:18). This means people will be all over the place when there's no clear sense of direction, no communicated vision. Many people are scatterbrained because they have no vision.

Never go before the Lord in prayer without a pen and piece of paper. Always be prepared to write down the things the Holy Spirit whispers into your heart.

CHAPTER 7: LIVE YOUR LIFE

RUN

Lastly, God told the prophet to write down the vision so that, after others see it, they'll be able to "run" with it. That means to make moves and put actions behind one's words. Don't just run with anything; run with God's vision. To run doesn't mean to walk; it means "move at a speed faster than a walk, never having both or all the feet on the ground at the same time" (Webster).

It's time to put some haste in your pace. That is what we mean by "beast mode". You're not treading lightly, moving slowly and delicately; you're moving rapaciously, steamrolling over anything that gets in your way, refusing to take no for an answer when you know God said it's yours. You're acting on every instruction that comes down from Heaven without hesitation. And as you do this, other people are watching in amazement as you walk through walls when there are no doors and accomplish the impossible. You have the green light from Heaven, and your foot is mashing the pedal to the metal. You're now in your element, your zone. You're doing what God created you to do.

*

You are unstoppable. That's how God designed you to be when pursuing that which rightfully belongs to you as your Kingdom inheritance. Don't stop. God called you to accomplish that dream, and He wants you to live the life of your dreams. There's something inside of you that's going to change your entire family, that's going to change your community, your whole neighborhood. You're about to experience greatness unlike anything you've ever imagined in your life. How do I know this? It's because God has you reading this book, and He laid this word of prophecy on my heart to deliver to you today; this isn't by coincidence or accident; it's by divine design that you're reading this. It was meant for you. Receive it!

And remember that all of this is not merely for yourself; it's for those coming after you. God is a generational God—He enjoys showering down generational blessings. So, where the devil brought generational curses and wreaked havoc in your family, God wants to undo that and make up for all that was lost and destroyed. God wants to redeem the time in your family's life, and He will use you to set things in motion.

LEGACY

You're about to leave a legacy behind for your children and grandchildren. Your entire household is about to be blessed. That's why I'm sharing all of this with you. Get ready for it because you're about to reverse the curse and change the course of your family members' lives. God wants you to be able to write that check and finance your dreams, send your children to the best schools and be a blessing to so many others. Yes, you are about to shift your family to another level. That was God's plan all the while. While you were busy discounting yourself because you didn't understand your value, worth and power, God declared that you were the key to it all the time. Assume your rightful place. Get ready to be the change agent in your family. And say this with me:

> "Today, my life has changed, and I will never be the same again! I'm going to greater heights and taking my family with me! Today, I know who I am,

CHAPTER 7: LIVE YOUR LIFE

my worth and my Kingdom assignment, and I will never settle for less again!"

If you are still wondering who the woman is sleeping with your husband, IT IS YOU! I am challenging you to discover who you are and walk in the gift that you are. Be all that God has birthed and created you to be!

If you find yourself in an abusive relationship or a marriage that is not healthy for you, get professional—and legal—help. See a counselor and get guidance for your next steps. Living a lie can be detrimental to your health and your family. Realize you are worth the fight—the fight for peace, sanity and success.

Be the best version of yourself. Know that you are great. God created you to be great! So don't waste time being contentious, engaging in back-biting, revenge, and other pettiness; be loving, kind, and encouraging towards others. You are a force to be reckoned with. You are gifted and graced for the best in life! So go and be about your Father's business!

Marriage is a gift from God but you have to know in your heart that you are where you belong! Love your husband but never forget about you. You are the "good thing" that God created.

WHO'S SLEEPING WITH YOUR HUSBAND?

PRAYER:

Dear Heavenly Father, I thank you for everything you shared with me in this book. I thank you that I know who I am. I cast off the garment of the old self and embrace who I am. I am fierce, bold, confident, beautiful, sexy, irresistible, powerful, creative, resourceful, victorious in all situations, more than a conqueror in Christ, adequate, capable, qualified by you, wealthy, powerful, influential, great, and blessed beyond measure. I receive who I am today. I thank you for revealing to me my true identity. Thank you for ordering my steps, giving me clarity of vision and making me an unstoppable force. I will live and not die, succeed and not fail, run and not walk, accomplish all you have called me to do on this earth, and bring glory to your name. I declare and decree these things today, and thank you that they're already established. I give you the praises, the glory and all of the honor this day, in Jesus' name, amen.

Speak Your Peace

Have you ever been in a bad situation where it seemed like the devil was attempting to stir up everything in your life, one where he was bringing contention, hurt and wounds, anger, fear and the works? During these turbulent times, you see yourself for who you are. How you respond during those moments reveals to you who you are. And so, the question remains, who is your husband sleeping with? Is he sleeping with a bitter, hurt, negative woman? Or is he sleeping with a confident, thriving and redeemed woman? It is apparent where you are in your emotional state when trying times come knocking at your door.

We must check and recheck ourselves constantly. But, we cannot do it alone. It only comes when we are honest with ourselves and willing to do the work to become healed and whole. Once we gain our healing, we can develop and foster healthy relationships. Only then will we see open doors and opportunities that will propel us to the next level in life and walk in true freedom and fulfillment.

God has made me and blessed me! He has clothed me

with His glory and has presented me as good. I am the gift! I am a woman of wisdom. I know what to do at the time I need to do it. I have divine insights. I protect my family from the enemy and intercede on their behalf. Because I have strong, unwavering faith in God and am rooted and grounded in love, I am victorious and a blessing to those around me.

I am fulfilling God's purpose for my life. Godly fruit abounds in every area of my life. I willingly and lovingly submit my will to God. I trust confidently in God to take care of me. God is my protector and my refuge. He has empowered me to fulfill my purpose. He has established me in His Word, His promises are manifested daily in my life, and I receive all I am entitled to under my covenant with God.

I am free from fear, doubt, and worry, and I renew my mind with the Word of God and rejuvenate my spirit through my daily fellowship with Jesus. I am a woman of power, great presence, high position and prosperity.

I look well to the ways of my home. The Lord will exalt me in due season, and my hands will always reap the fruit of increase. In Jesus' Name, amen!

Dr. Jeri Godhigh is available for interviews, appearances and speaking engagements. Contact Josie's Girls Lead | 888-413-7337

Made in the USA
Columbia, SC
13 July 2025